D0468251

BRAR'

NO LONGER PROPE
SEATTLE PUBLIC LIBRARY

Hi **5E** !
(name or unit number)

I just made **DINNER** and
(meal)

I have extra **FRENCH ONION TOAST** .
(toast)

You hungry? I could stop by **LATER TONIGHT** .
(time)

with it for a **PETER SELLERS MARATHON** .
(coffee/ nibble/ romp/ nightcap/ movie)

Knock whenever.

xo **JILL**

Better on TOAST

Better on TOAST

HAPPINESS ON A SLICE OF BREAD

70 IRRESISTIBLE RECIPES

Jill Donenfeld

WM
WILLIAM MORROW
An Imprint of HarperCollinsPublishers

BETTER ON TOAST. Copyright © 2015 by Jill A. Donenfeld. All rights reserved. Printed in the United States of America. No part of this book may be used or reproduced in any manner whatsoever without written permission except in the case of brief quotations embodied in critical articles and reviews. For information address HarperCollins Publishers, 195 Broadway, New York, NY 10007.

HarperCollins books may be purchased for educational, business, or sales promotional use. For information please email the Special Markets Department at SPsales@harpercollins.com.

FIRST EDITION

Designed by Pagnozzi Creative
Photographs by John Von Pamer

Library of Congress Cataloging-in-Publication Data has been applied for.

ISBN 978-0-06-232904-2

15 16 17 18 19   OV/QG   10 9 8 7 6 5 4 3 2 1

When you know how to listen, everybody is the guru.
—RAM DASS

 To Jane Frye and the interns since the beginning

contents

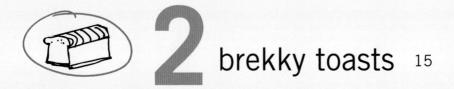

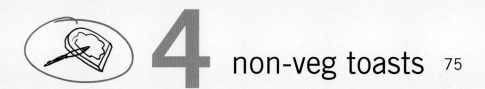
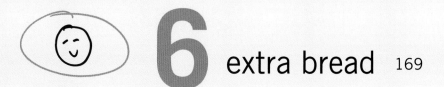

introduction

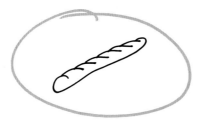

James Beard said, "Good bread is the most fundamentally satisfying of all foods; and good bread with fresh butter, the greatest of feasts." It's the most basic, the most coveted, and the most craved. It's the tradition that brings us to the table, how we start the day, and the happy beginning of many other meals as well.

One of my first jobs in New York was as a waitress at a now-closed restaurant on the Lower East Side. Because of that job, I speak of being a waitress as "my favorite job." I loved being in the hot seat, with food, beverages, and the perfect pacing of a first date all on my shoulders.

The best part of that job was the bread and butter.

Julie and Tasha, the chef-owners, made herb butter, and it was part of the waitresses' job to scrape it into little dishes, sprinkle them with salt, and drop them at our tables after guests had placed an order. When the butter was at the right temperature and the Pullman loaf was fresh and sticky, it was impossible to go a shift without being asked by every table for more of both.

The customers were happy, but I was happier, owing to my discovery of the panini press.

After setting up the bread service, I'd spread any leftover butter onto as many pieces of bread as I could cover. I'd pop them in the panini press and grill up some perfect toast. This would sustain me until shift drink, when I'd make some more. That taste—hot, crusty bread, a little soft in the center, with a layer of buttery grilled herbs—put me on the path that resulted in this book.

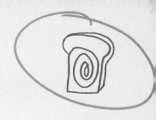

1 bread

Toast

Toasting Techniques

Quinoa-Millet Bread

Variations

I n New York City, I'm surrounded by superb bread. Breads Bakery and Maison Kayser aren't only in my dreams; they are in Union Square. Bien Cuit and Runner & Stone in Brooklyn are worth a subway ride. There are the classics like semolina raisin at Amy's Bread, pizza bianca at Sullivan Street Bakery, baguette at Balthazar. Even if I'm doing one-stop shopping, Dean & DeLuca, Agata & Valentina, Citarella, and Whole Foods all have great selections.

And when I'm not in New York City, great bread, thankfully, is in abundance. The Whole Foods in Boulder, Colorado, has a tremendous selection. Huckleberry in Los Angeles does great English muffins. Servatii in Cincinnati has unrivaled pretzel bread. There's a mom-and-pop bakery in most small towns. Fantastic bread—or at least pretty great bread—isn't terribly difficult to find.

There's baguette, miche, Pullman, and ciabatta for tasty neutrals; brioche, challah, and bread laden with raisins and cranberries and cinnamon for sweetness. There's grainy bread for texture and rye for tang. There's bread with olives, walnuts, rosemary, and Parmesan if you want your slices savory.

I have a bread-making friend whom I consider a magician, but I generally don't make bread myself. If, like me, you don't have time to hone your sorcery, then purchase the highest-quality bread that you can find. My recipes are simple so it pays to buy the good stuff. Bread is a fine thing to be left to the pro bakers.

TOAST

It's not rocket science we're talking about here. It's not even molecular gastronomy. It's not specific to any technique, culture, or diet. Food tastes better when it's eaten on a piece of hot, crispy bread. There's something primal about it. We break bread to commune. It satisfies a physical hunger as well as the desire to share.

Bread alone is beautiful but not satisfying. A full loaf of bread can be a dangerous thing, eaten easily and accidentally in a single sitting. But if I top a few slices with some salmon or avocado or even simply sliced radishes, then I'm perfectly sated and not wrecked.

A toast, aka a tartine, open-faced sandwich, or *smørrebrød* (if you want to get fancy when addressing a single-slice serving stacked high), is universal and portable. A toast can be contained, held with one hand while texting a buddy, writing a thank-you note, typing a work email, or applying mascara with the other hand.

It's seductive and satisfying in its simplicity, but toppings can also get creative. A toast is a choose-your-own-adventure in culinary form. Start with baguette, and French doors open. If you start with brown bread, consider something creamy and maybe with a little brine. Want to toast the bread dry or sear it with mayonnaise? Slice it thin; keep it thick? There are so many ways to make it into exactly what you want—and so many ways to use what you already have stocked in the pantry. It can be breakfast with an egg. It can be lunch and dinner. It can be a snack or an appetizer.

I keep it pretty simple, paring down ingredients and techniques. I rely on layering flavors. These recipes are flexible, pointers with room for improvisation—I give substitutions, shortcuts, and tips. Toasts can be made by anyone, no matter the level of expertise or the type of kitchen. And they can be eaten anytime, anywhere. Hot, herby bread on the Lower East Side was my primer (see the introduction) and I still believe there's nothing greater than sliced bread—except, it turns out, when it's toast.

Here, let's toast to toast!

oil

Mayo

Parmesan

spice

grilled

butter

herbs

TOASTING TECHNIQUES

The recipes in this book will be enjoyable with any type of bread, toasted any way, but the following techniques are referenced throughout. Additionally, some of the recipes suggest following these toasting techniques that use ingredients and infusions—think rosemary oil (page 96) and thyme butter (page 141)—that get made for specific recipes. There's more than one way to toast.

plain old toast

Pan-Toasting Method

1. Heat a generous amount of olive oil (enough to cover the bottom of the pan)* in a cast-iron skillet (ideally).

2. Turn the heat on high. When the oil is hot, place the bread in the pan. Turn down the heat if the bread begins to brown too fast. Let toast until golden, 2 to 3 minutes, then flip and repeat on the other side.

3. Finish with a bit of big flaky salt if desired.

*If you really want flavor, use enough oil to cover the toast halfway up and toast like that. That's the heavy-soaking technique.

Spice Pan-Toasting Method

1. Heat a generous amount of olive oil (enough to cover the bottom of the pan) in a cast-iron skillet (ideally).

2. Turn the heat on high.

3. Place the bread in the oil, then turn it over with tongs to oil both sides. Sprinkle onto the bread the spices or dried herbs of your choice—for example, Old Bay, dried oregano, garlic powder, dry mustard, dried dill, or delicious ras el hanout (usually a combination of cardamom, clove, cinnamon, ground chile pepper, coriander, cumin, pepper, paprika, fenugreek, and turmeric). Damn good on toast.

4. When the oil is hot, flip the bread so it is spice side down. Add spices, dried herbs, and so on to the other side and toast until golden, 2 to 3 minutes.

Mayonnaise or Butter Pan-Toasting Method

1. Spread mayonnaise* or butter evenly on both sides of the slice of bread.

2. Heat a cast-iron skillet (ideally) over medium heat. When the oil is hot, place the bread in the pan and toast until golden brown, 2 to 3 minutes.

3. Flip the bread and repeat on the other side.

*I prefer mayonnaise to butter because it gives toast an ideal golden crust. But in recipes that call for butter, it's best not to substitute mayo, as it saves you from pulling out another ingredient and keeps the flavor consistent.

Parmesan Pan-Toasting Method

1. Spread a very thin layer of butter evenly on both sides of a bread slice. Smash freshly grated Parmesan into one side of the toast.

2. Heat a cast-iron skillet (ideally) over medium heat. When the pan is hot, place the bread in the pan, Parmesan side down, and toast until golden brown, 1 to 2 minutes.

3. Sprinkle the top with Parmesan, smashing it in so it adheres, and flip the bread. Toast another 1 to 2 minutes, or until the cheese on the bottom is melted and crisp but not burned.

Oven-Toasting Method

1. Preheat the oven to 350°F.

2. Lay the slices of bread on a parchment-lined baking sheet.

3. Brush, drizzle, or rub the bread with olive oil, butter, or mayonnaise to coat both sides. Toast in the oven until golden brown, 5 to 10 minutes, depending on the desired darkness.

Herb Oven-Toasting Method

1. Preheat the oven to 350°F.

2. Blend a generous amount of olive oil or butter with herbs of your choice (such as chopped basil and thyme, rosemary, or chopped sage—or all four) using a blender, an immersion blender, or a food processor.

3. Lay the slices of bread on a parchment-lined baking sheet.

4. Brush, drizzle, or rub the bread with the herb oil or butter on both sides. Toast in the oven until golden brown, 5 to 10 minutes, depending on the desired darkness.

Grilling Method

1. Heat a grill* or grill pan over medium heat.

2. Brush the bread with olive oil on both sides. Grill until golden and dark grill marks form, 2 to 3 minutes.

3. Flip and repeat on the other side.

*You can use a grill with herb oil and even Parmesan, too. But apply Parmesan to only one side of the toast, after you've grilled a side and flipped.

Plain Old Toast

If you don't want to introduce a fat element into your toasting technique, heat sliced bread in the oven, toaster, or toaster oven until it reaches the desired golden color; 350°F is a neutral temperature that will allow you to keep an eye on your bread. Toast for 5 to 10 minutes, depending on the desired doneness. In a toaster, err on the 5-minute side. Adjust the light–dark spectrum accordingly.

A FEW TOASTED POINTS

If you're toasting a lot of bread at once, opt for oven toasting; or if you pan-toast in batches, keep your bread warm in the oven at 200°F, tented loosely with tinfoil (leaving room to breathe). The thickness of bread slices affects fat saturation and toasting time—you want your bread to be sturdy but not over-powering of the toppings. If you're toasting up some very crusty loaves, don't toast too long—you want your toast to give a little but not be too unwieldy to eat in front of others. Softer breads (with softer crusts) can get thicker slices—they have a more soakable texture. And when it comes to slicing, a ser-rated knife is the samurai sword of choice. It makes for a cleaner, easier motion.

TOASTING : NUTS

Toasting nuts is as easy as toasting bread! And I call for them a lot in this book. Use any saucepan you're going to use for the recipe. Put the nuts in the pan, turn the heat to medium-high, and move the nuts around with a spatula or spoon. They will toast after 4 to 8 minutes (faster for pine nuts—and actually any small nut). As long as you watch them and they don't burn, you did it right! Once they're toasted, spread them on a plate or towel to cool.

AN OUTSTANDING, VERSATILE BREAD WITHOUT THE G-WORD

I had a little get-together. It was impromptu, so I bought three breads and one type of cracker and then did some soft cheeses and salmon roe and marinated tomatoes and olives and put them all out like a build-your-own deal. It was more about champagne than anything else, so there wasn't a ton of pressure to perform. But there was a guest who couldn't eat gluten, so I made an effort to buy some bread that wouldn't kill her.

Then it turned out that that bread was good. And everyone was devouring it without knowing that it was gluten-free. It just happened to be the tastiest loaf (within an excel-lent selection of cranberry walnut, ciabatta, and fennel seed crackers).

There's been a lot of talk about gluten. Gluten, the thing that makes bread chewy and airy and awesome, forms when the proteins found in wheat flour mix with water. It's the magic. It's also the thing that makes many people ill.

Because it seemed weird to not include a recipe for bread in a book that rests on the very stuff, here's one bread recipe that doesn't compete with the myriad loaves all over the world made by bakers who've dedicated their lives to perfecting their witchcraft.

It's gluten-free, which is hard to find a delicious version of at most groceries and bakeries. But just think of it as a yummy, homemade, versatile loaf, not something to make only for people with gluten-free diets. It isn't labor intensive, and you can order the ingredients online. So try it—at least once.

IT'S ABOUT WHAT GOES INTO IT, NOT WHAT GETS LEFT OUT.

Quinoa-Millet Bread

This bread uses brown rice and quinoa flours instead of wheat flour. The only "scary" ingredient in this recipe is xanthan gum, which is a sugar-fermented plant bacterium that gets ground into a powder to act as an emulsifier, thickener, and gluten imitator. Don't be afraid.

This bread holds up when toasted, grilled, fried, and rubbed with garlic; it's fantastic with all the toasting methods. It's highly absorbent and very forgiving. It serves as a base for making sweet and savory versions and stays soft for 4 to 5 days.

2 teaspoons active dry yeast	¾ cup potato starch
1½ cups warm water (between 90°F and 100°F)*	½ cup millet
	4 teaspoons xanthan gum
1 tablespoon honey	2 teaspoons salt
1½ cups brown rice flour	¼ cup olive oil
½ cup quinoa flour	3 large eggs plus 3 large egg whites
¼ cup flaxseed meal	1 teaspoon apple cider vinegar

1. In a small bowl, combine the yeast, water, and honey. Let sit for 10 minutes. It should get foamy.

2. Meanwhile, to a medium saucepan over medium-high heat, add the brown rice flour, quinoa flour, and flaxseed meal. Stir until tan and toasty, 7 to 10 minutes. Let cool, then mix in the potato starch, millet, xanthan gum, and salt.

3. In a medium bowl, whisk the oil, eggs, egg whites, and cider vinegar together.

4. Transfer the flour mixture to a standing mixer. Add the yeast mixture and pulse a few times until combined. Add the oil mixture and continue to mix for 2 to 3 minutes (or mix by hand for 8 to 10 minutes) until a smooth dough forms.

*Microwave room-temp water for about 1 minute to reach 100°F . . . it should feel like a not-that-hot hot tub when you dip your finger in. If the water is too hot, you risk killing the yeast, which will keep the bread from rising.

5. Lightly oil a 10-inch loaf pan. Transfer the dough to the prepared loaf pan. Let rise in a warm place for 1 to 2 hours, until doubled in size.

6. Preheat the oven to 350°F.

7. Bake until the bread is golden brown and baked through, 45 minutes to 1 hour. The internal temperature should be 160°F if you have a thermometer; otherwise, just vibe it—stick a toothpick in the center to see if it comes out clean, or press the top to see if it's bouncy. Cool before slicing.

↳ THIS IS GOOD.

VARIATIONS

Sweet:

Add 3 tablespoons honey, 1 tablespoon ground cinnamon, and ½ cup raisins in step 4 before adding the oil mixture. This version rises more than the others because of the extra sugar, which feeds the yeast.

Savory:

Add ½ cup chopped Kalamata olives and ¼ cup julienned sun-dried tomatoes in step 4 before adding the oil mixture. Let it rise a little longer to ensure fluffiness.

Sultry:

Add 2 tablespoons chopped rosemary, ½ cup grated Parmesan, and ½ cup chopped walnuts in step 4 before adding the oil mixture. The cheese really binds the dough; this is the closest version to bread with gluten.

2 brekky toasts

← MAKE A HOLE
IN THE BREAD.
CRACK THE EGG
INTO THE HOLE
WHEN PAN-TOASTING.

Avocado Classic

Super simple but perhaps the gateway drug to a book full of toast, the avotoast is a way of life. I first experienced it at Cafe Gitane in SoHo in 2002. There's since been a proliferation; no one's complaining. Give yourself this gift as often as possible.

2 ripe avocados, pitted and peeled

3 to 4 tablespoons freshly squeezed lemon juice

¼ teaspoon salt

4 ½-inch-thick slices highly grainy bread, pan-toasted (see page 6)

¼ teaspoon red chili pepper flakes

2 tablespoons olive oil

1 lemon, quartered

1. In a medium bowl, using a fork, half mash the avocados with the lemon juice and salt.

2. Top the toasts with the citrusy avocado. Sprinkle with chili flakes and a drizzle of oil.

3. Serve each toast with a lemon quarter, to be squeezed aggressively at the table.

Smoked Trout and Grapefruit

One of the nicest things a boyfriend has done for me was to break into my apartment. The guy busted in, supremed enough grapefruit to fill a quart container, cleaned up his mess, and exited unseen. A supremed slice of fruit is simple decadence, and it's a pain: Juice. Gets. Everywhere. Never mind all that juice (or awaiting another boyfriend break-in); here is the lazy lady supreme. It provides a similar effect, plus it's lawful and especially convenient when preparing breakfast.

1 grapefruit

¼ cup pitted Kalamata olives

2 teaspoons agave nectar

2 tablespoons olive oil

1 teaspoon lemon juice

2 tablespoons crème fraîche

4 ¼-inch-thick slices whole wheat, rye, or spelt bread, oven-toasted (see page 8)

¼ cup small-diced peeled cucumber

4 ounces smoked trout

1 teaspoon lemon zest

1. **Lazy lady supreme** the grapefruit by slicing off both ends, then the rest of the peel, removing all the pith. Slice in half, top to bottom. Then slice into half-moons. Pull the segments apart. You'll use half the grapefruit.

2. In a food processor or with an immersion blender, mix the olives, agave nectar, oil, and lemon juice until smooth. Transfer to a bowl and mix in the crème fraîche.

3. Spread the olive crème on the toasts. Lay on the grapefruit sections. Top with pieces of cucumber dice and smoked trout. Sprinkle with the lemon zest.

Lazy Lady

Want to pickle? Sub out the cucumbers for fennel. In a small saucepan, boil ½ cup water, ½ cup champagne vinegar, 1 tablespoon salt, and 2 tablespoons sugar. Very thinly slice 1 fennel bulb and place it in a bowl with some fresh tarragon leaves. Pour the hot pickling liquid over the fennel. Let cool, drain, and use. Pickled fennel lasts at least a month in the fridge. Alternatively, don't drain it: the longer it sits, the more potent it gets.

Togarashi Egg Salad

So many people are egg salad haters. Enough is enough. Take two steps forward by taking one step back. *Stop* hating on country club food and *start* spicing it up with shichimi togarashi, a wondrous Asian spice blend that combines sesame seeds, orange peel, red pepper, and ginger. And drink a cup of shiso tea along with it.

8 eggs

2 tablespoons mayonnaise

1 tablespoon rice vinegar

¼ teaspoon shichimi togarashi

Pinch of freshly ground black pepper

½ teaspoon salt

1 celery stalk, cut into small dice (about ½ cup)

1 cup arugula

4 ½-inch slices seedy bread, lightly oven-toasted (see page 8)

2 shiso leaves, julienned

4 shiso leaves for tea

1. Hard-boil the eggs: Fill a medium pot with 1 inch of water and bring it to a boil. Carefully place the eggs in, cover the pot, and cook for 9 to 10 minutes. Drain the hot water and run the eggs under cold water for 30 seconds.*

2. Peel the eggs and place 6 of them in a medium bowl. Add only the whites of the remaining 2 eggs and discard the yolks or reserve for another use. Add the mayonnaise, vinegar, togarashi, pepper, and salt. Mash with the back of a fork—but don't overmash. Mix in the celery.

3. Divide the arugula among the toasts and top with egg salad. Sprinkle julienned shiso on top.

This is like the guru technique (page 38) except the eggs are cooked a little longer to firm up the center.

Shiso Tea

Make a cup of shiso tea by steeping a shiso leaf in boiling water—*et voilà*!

Oyster Omelet

An oyster omelet is double-O heaven. Especially with ketchup, and yet I used to be ashamed.
I like ketchup on my eggs, slathering it like a thick layer of butter across an English muffin.
I like my eggs to get slippery in the crimson sauce. Many people are grossed out. Whatever.
Ketchup is our nation's sriracha, and the two mixed together with a splash of soy sauce takes
on a new meaning that inspires unapologetic use. No need to go undercover.

2 tablespoons ketchup

2 teaspoons sriracha

Splash of soy sauce (optional)

½ tablespoon unsalted butter

1 large egg

2 large egg whites

4 or 5 fresh or jarred shucked oysters

¼ cup chopped watercress

1 English muffin, oven-toasted
(see page 8)

Freshly ground black pepper

1. Combine the ketchup, sriracha, and soy
   sauce (if using) in a small bowl. Set
   aside.

2. In a small pan* over medium heat,
   melt the butter, swirling to cover the
   pan.

3. Beat the egg and egg whites in a
   bowl. Add the eggs to the pan,
   without stirring. After a minute,
   add the oysters.

*If you want to make a baby omelet to go on half an
English muffin, mini Lodge cast-iron skillets will
come in very handy—they're nearly the perfect size
for English muffins. Just divide the ingredients and
prepare half at a time. Move over, Egg McMuffins.

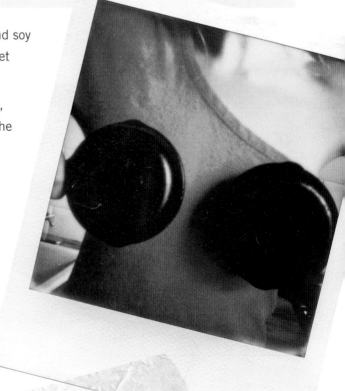

4. Once the eggs begin to set, 2 to 3 minutes more, add the watercress. Let set completely, then fold the omelet in thirds. Flip the omelet, cook 1 to 3 more minutes, and cut it in half.

5. Slather the toasted English muffin with the ketchup mixture, top with the omelet, and sprinkle with pepper.

YOU HEARD IT HERE SECOND: SMOKED SALMON

Nothing new—just real, real good. Smoked salmon. Size, shape, and flavor . . . ideal on toast. There are more variations than a page can handle, but for the record, here are a few on my mixtape.

Smoked salmon + avocado + splash of freshly squeezed orange juice

Smoked salmon + capers + black olives + lemon

Smoked salmon + shaved radishes + radish greens

Smoked salmon + scrambled eggs + onions

Smoked salmon + ricotta + cucumber

Smoked salmon rillettes (see opposite page) + pickles

Smoked salmon + herbed goat cheese (see page 57)

Smoked salmon + cream cheese + grainy sweet mustard

Smoked salmon + hard-boiled egg + butter

Smoked salmon + Togarashi Egg Salad (see page 23)

Smoked salmon + sweet pea puree (see page 124)

Smoked salmon + leftover cold white pizza

Rillettes

1 tablespoon olive oil

1 shallot, chopped

1 tablespoon white wine

1 tablespoon chopped fresh chives

1 tablespoon crème fraîche

1 tablespoon mayonnaise

4 ounces smoked salmon, chopped

1 teaspoon lemon zest

1 tablespoon freshly squeezed lemon juice

Salt and freshly ground black pepper to taste

Heat a small pan over medium heat with the oil. Add the shallot and sauté until translucent, 5 to 7 minutes. Deglaze with the wine. Transfer to a medium bowl and let cool. Add the chives, crème fraîche, mayonnaise, salmon, lemon zest, lemon juice, and salt and pepper. Mix up well.

Harissa Scramble

I learned this recipe around the time that I started getting very into bottarga, having befriended (and then become business partners with) a Canadian Tunisian living in lower Manhattan through one of those friend-of-a-friend-of-a-friend New York moments. He had learned to make it from his Tunisian grandmother, making him a passionate artisan and one who never tires of the taste, both traits happily infectious. The cured roe of mullet (more on bottarga on page 111) can take the place of any savory enricher (such as Parmesan or stock), and putting it on scrambled eggs with harissa makes for a trifecta of creamy, spicy, and salty. Think of it as if a twenty-four-hour diner offered a North African egg option next to its Western omelet.

4 large eggs

¼ cup chopped scallions

2 to 3 tablespoons harissa

2 tablespoons whole milk

½ teaspoon freshly ground black pepper

1 tablespoon unsalted butter

2 garlic cloves, minced

4 ½-inch-thick slices sourdough sesame bread, pan-toasted with butter (see page 7)

1 ounce bottarga (about half of 1 small lobe)

2 tablespoons chopped fresh parsley

1. In a small bowl, mix the eggs, scallions, harissa, milk, and pepper. Beat until combined.

2. In a medium pan over medium heat, melt the butter and sauté the garlic for 1 minute, until the garlic is softened.

3. Pour the mixture into the pan and cook the eggs, turning them over with a fork, until they scramble evenly.

4. Top the toasts with the scrambled eggs. Using a Microplane, vigorously zest the bottarga over the eggs. Sprinkle with the parsley.

Bacon and Date

Bacon is best as a special treat. That's why this bacon gets matched with sweet ricotta and sugary pecans. It's an easy toast to entertain with—make a big batch of ricotta and the whole package of bacon and let your friends build their own.

4 Medjool dates, very finely chopped

2 tablespoons maple syrup

1 cup ricotta (see page 130)

4 thick-cut bacon strips, halved crosswise

2 tablespoons brown sugar

¼ cup chopped pecans

6 ¼-inch-thick slices whole wheat Pullman bread or sourdough, oven-toasted (see page 8)

1. In a small bowl, mix the dates, maple syrup, and ricotta. Set aside.

2. In a medium pan over medium heat, cook the bacon until crispy, 7 to 10 minutes. Lay the bacon on a paper towel to dry.

3. Add the sugar and pecans to the bacon fat and cook, stirring, until the nuts are toasted, about 3 minutes.

4. To assemble the toasts, spread the ricotta mixture on each piece of toast, top with 1 or 2 pieces of bacon, and sprinkle with the pecans.

Madagascar Banana

I'm thinking about you. About your love of avocado toast. But might you be craving a sweet change? Mmm . . . Living in Madagascar was a very sweet change. I learned about eating avocados with bananas—both grow in abundance there. It's weird until you do it for yourself. Like you, I swoon over straight avocado toast, too (see page 16 for my Classic). And change is tough. But stick with me, kid. Soon you'll be on the next flight to Antananarivo.

2 tablespoons sliced almonds

2 tablespoons shredded unsweetened coconut, *if you have it around*

½ very ripe banana

1 ripe avocado, pitted and peeled

½ teaspoon lemon juice

¼ teaspoon salt

4 ½-inch-thick slices whole-grain bread or ½-inch-thick slices Quinoa-Millet Bread (see page 11), oven-toasted (see page 8)

3 tablespoons crumbled feta or cottage cheese

Pinch of freshly ground black pepper

1. In a small pan over medium heat, toast the almonds and coconut (if using) until browned, stirring often, about 4 minutes.

2. In a medium bowl, use a fork to mash together the banana, avocado, lemon juice, and salt until smooth.

3. Spread the mixture evenly onto each piece of toast.

(continued)

4. Top with a sprinkle of crumbled feta or a dollop of cottage cheese. Sprinkle with the pepper, toasted almonds, and coconut (if using).

Apricot-Stuffed French Toast

MAKES 4 FRENCH TOASTS

Apricots are a very seasonal item—end-of-summer jewels happily in abundance around my birthday. If you aren't making this for me to ring in another year, or you just want French toast in another season, make this recipe using mango (fresh or frozen), bananas, or apples.

5 fresh apricots, pitted and cut into ½-inch-thick slices

¼ cup plus 1 tablespoon turbinado sugar

½ teaspoon grated fresh ginger

1 teaspoon lemon zest

2 teaspoons freshly squeezed lemon juice

4 2-inch-thick slices challah bread

3 large eggs

3 cups whole milk

½ teaspoon pure vanilla extract

½ teaspoon ground cinnamon

¼ teaspoon ground cardamom

3 tablespoons unsalted butter

1. Preheat the oven to 350°F and line a large baking sheet with parchment paper.

2. In a small bowl, combine the apricots, 1 tablespoon sugar, ginger, lemon zest, and lemon juice. Refrigerate for at least 30 minutes and up to 2 hours.

3. Using a small serrated knife, such as a steak knife, cut a slit in each bread slice. Cut into the bread horizontally as deep as you can without cutting through to the other side, leaving ¼ inch on both the left and right sides. Think *pita pocket.*

4. Stuff the macerated apricots into the pockets, reserving a few slices.

5. In a large bowl, whisk together the eggs, milk, the remaining ¼ cup sugar, the vanilla, cinnamon, and cardamom.

6. Dip a piece of stuffed bread into the batter. Let the bread sit until it's heavy with the batter but not falling apart, 10 to 15 seconds. If the bread is not submerged, flip after 8 to 10 seconds.

(continued)

7. Heat a large skillet or griddle over high heat. Add some of the butter and swirl to cover the pan, then reduce the heat to low. Add the bread and cook until golden, 3 to 5 minutes on each side, then lay the French toast on the prepared baking sheet. Repeat to cook the rest of the French toast, refreshing the butter in between batches to keep the toast from sticking.

8. Put the baking sheet in the oven to finish cooking the toasts, baking for 5 to 10 minutes, or until it firms up a bit.

9. Serve with the reserved apricots on top.

I'M GETTING HOT

- If your skillet gets too hot, it may be necessary to turn the heat down or off while you finish the toast. Cast-iron models retain heat very well.

- If you want to make the French toast a little ahead of time, you can store the toasts loosely covered with foil in a 200°F oven for up to an hour.

Green Guru Eggs

My guru showed me the way to make a perfect hard-boiled egg. The guru egg is still a little runny at the very center. *That's a good guru!*

3 large eggs

1 tablespoon freshly squeezed lemon juice

2 tablespoons olive oil

½ teaspoon salt

½ ripe avocado, pitted and peeled

2 tablespoons chopped fresh chives, plus a few more for garnish

8 to 12 Little Gem lettuce leaves

4 ½-inch-thick slices sourdough bread, pan-toasted in mayonnaise (see page 7)

Freshly ground black pepper

1. Hard-boil the eggs using the guru method (see sidebar). Slice the eggs into rounds, about 5 per egg.

2. Using an immersion blender or a food processor, puree the lemon juice, oil, salt, avocado, and chives until smooth. Add a little water if needed. You want a smooth, thin consistency.

3. Top the toasts with 2 to 3 lettuce leaves each and the egg slices. Drizzle with the green sauce. Garnish with chives and pepper and serve immediately.

HARD-BOILED EGGS
Guru-Style

Fill a saucepan with 1 inch of water and bring it to a boil over medium-high heat. Carefully place the eggs in, cover the pot, and cook for 7 to 8 minutes, depending on the desired runniness. Drain the hot water and run the eggs under cold water for 30 seconds. Peel.

Tomatillo Egg

Babin' ain't easy. And this is one smokin' toast. You could serve this on tortillas, of course. And adding cotija cheese would be great, too. You'll have extra sauce and black bean mash

... So you can have eggs for days.

8 ½-inch-thick slices sourdough bread or rye miche	½ teaspoon salt
5 garlic cloves, halved	½ teaspoon freshly ground black pepper
Olive oil	1 15-ounce can black beans, rinsed and drained
10 medium fresh tomatillos, husked, or 1 13-ounce can tomatillos, drained	1 ripe avocado, pitted and peeled
1 cup roughly chopped cilantro	2 tablespoons freshly squeezed lime juice
1 jalapeño, seeded	8 large eggs
1 cup chopped white onion	¼ cup crème fraîche

1. Rub the bread vigorously with the garlic (reserve the garlic). Heat a large skillet over medium heat, add the oil, and pan-toast the bread (see page 6).

2. To make the tomatillo sauce, boil the tomatillos in salted water until soft, about 10 minutes. (If using canned tomatillos, skip boiling them.) Using a blender, puree the tomatillos, the reserved garlic, ¾ cup of the cilantro, the jalapeño, onion, salt, and pepper until smooth. Add a little water to thin it (⅓ cup, roughly).* Set aside.

3. In a medium bowl, mash the black beans, avocado, and lime juice, leaving the mixture a little chunky. Spread about ⅓ cup on each toast and set aside.

*Idea! Instead of boiling the tomatillos, you can roast them if you feel like turning on the oven. Just peel off the papery covering and roast at 400°F for 10 to 12 minutes.

(continued)

4. Heat the tomatillo sauce in a large pan over high heat. When hot, crack 2 or 3 eggs (don't crowd them) into the sauce and cook until the whites are opaque but the yolks are still runny, about 4 minutes. Season to taste with salt and pepper. Remove each egg with a slotted spoon and place it on a toast.

5. Let the sauce cook down to thicken slightly, about 5 minutes. Remove from the heat, stir in the crème fraîche, and pour about ¼ cup over each toast. Garnish with the remaining cilantro and another hit of pepper.

FILL YOUR PLATE

Have the toasts with the black bean–avocado mash and serve eggs on the side to make a full-plate brekky.

Ricotta Part I: Lavender Ricotta

MAKES 1 TO 1½ CUPS RICOTTA, BUT DOUBLE IT UP, NO PROBLEM

A toast basic every enthusiast should know: ricotta is a big deal in Toast Town. Put another way, there are a few things that I do on a regular basis: I do twenty push-ups almost every day. I write thank-you notes. I carry a headlamp in my bag and often a Leatherman tool, too. I eat chewable vitamin C. I can't get it together to routinely floss, but I do make ricotta. It is stupidly easy to make and completely outstanding. It's versatile, essentially foolproof, and total princess food. Eat it in the morning: you'll feel like royalty all day. It's also less expensive than buying it and way, way more impressive.

Make lavender ricotta because it's just that extra bit of brag power. Top it with a few goodies and you'll make a loyal puppy out of the person you're feeding.

1 quart whole milk

½ cup heavy cream

½ teaspoon salt

2 tablespoons lavender

1 1-inch-long fresh ginger knob, peeled and thinly sliced

2 tablespoons freshly squeezed lemon juice

you need cheesecloth

1. Bring the milk, cream, salt, lavender, and ginger to a boil in a medium saucepan over medium heat, stirring often so that the mixture doesn't burn, about 10 minutes, then remove from the heat.

2. Line a sieve or mesh strainer with cheesecloth and place it over a medium bowl. Pour the mixture through the cheesecloth to strain out the lavender and ginger and discard them.

3. Return the infused milk to the pan and place the pan over medium-low heat. Add the lemon juice and bring to a simmer, stirring constantly. After about 2 minutes, the mixture will start to curdle—the solids will start to pull away from the liquid.

(continued)

The longer you allow the mixture to curdle, the harder your cheese will be.

4. Line the sieve or mesh strainer with new cheesecloth and place it over the bowl. Pour the mixture through the cheesecloth and set it aside to strain for about 1 hour. (Remember, strain time affects consistency and yield, too. Proceed according to your preference.) Discard the liquid* and transfer the ricotta to a bowl. Chill until cold and eat within 3 days.†

*Cook brown rice using your lavender whey. Whey rice is way good.
†If you aren't in the mood to make ricotta, buy it and proceed with your toasts (to the right). If you're looking to cut a few calories, you could even use cottage cheese. You're still a princess. As much as I love ricotta, I just want you to be happy.

For lavender ricotta adventures, see opposite page.

Another awesome use for lavender:

Add it to the pot when boiling shrimp. Lavender, bay leaves, sugar, and salt turn a simple shrimp cocktail into an elegant, nuanced dish, or check out the sweet toast on page 178.

LAVENDER RICOTTA

FIG
HONEY
PEPPER

PEACHES
BASIL
HONEY

CHERRY JAM
TOASTED PISTACHIOS

STRAWBERRIES
BALSAMIC REDUCTION

Ricotta Bonus Round: Jam-Swirled Ricotta Pancakes

MAKES ABOUT 12 5-INCH PANCAKES

I was just thinking . . . You're going to have all that ricotta, so you might want to make ricotta pancakes. You could use the quinoa flour you have from the Quinoa-Millet Bread (page 11). This is a good chance to put that to use. Then you can tout this brekky as gluten-free while you bask in the efficiency of your pantry cleaning. And the batter freezes well, so it's great for laid-back entertaining.

For these jam-swirled beauties, I like the idea of using orange marmalade with the tarragon ricotta (see page 131) or peach jam with the lavender ricotta (see page 43). You could also do this savory with plain-made ricotta—add chopped asparagus and grated Parmesan (and omit the sugar in the recipe below).

1½ teaspoons lemon zest

2 tablespoons turbinado sugar

¾ cup all-purpose or quinoa flour

½ teaspoon baking powder

¼ teaspoon salt

1 cup lavender ricotta (see page 43), tarragon ricotta (see page 131), or plain ricotta (see page 130)

3 large eggs, separated

½ cup whole milk

⅓ cup jam of your choice—my mom suggests blackberry

2 tablespoons unsalted butter

1. In a small bowl, mix the lemon zest with the sugar. Do this before anything else (even the night before) so the sugar gets citrusy.

2. In a medium bowl, mix the flour, baking powder, salt, and lemon sugar.

3. In a large bowl, whisk together the ricotta, egg yolks, and milk.

4. In a small saucepan or in a small bowl in the microwave, heat up the jam, stirring to make sure it's a bit fluid, about 20 seconds. Set aside.

5. With an electric mixer, beat the egg whites until stiff (this is much easier in a cold metal bowl).

6. Add the flour mixture to the ricotta mixture and whisk until just combined. Fold in the egg white fluff, working slowly so as not to deflate it.

7. Melt 1 teaspoon of the butter in a pan over medium heat, swirling to cover the bottom of the pan. Add a few dollops of batter, taking care not to crowd the pancakes. Cook for 3 to 4 minutes, until bubbles hit the tops of the pancakes and the bottoms are getting browned. Just before flipping the pancakes, drop a small spoonful of jam in the center of each one and gently drag it around in a swirl with a knife. Flip and cook 2 to 3 minutes more. Refresh the pan with butter between batches so the pancakes do not stick to the pan. Continue to make pancakes until all of the batter is used.

3 hors d'oeuvre toasts

Scallop Carpaccio with Kalamata-Orange Relish and Lemon Aioli

Nectarine Caprese

Grilled Hearts of Palm with Saffron Hummus

Herbed Goat Cheese and Grilled Vegetables

Roe Out

Edamame Basil

Hot Miso Crab

Pesto Swirl

Kale and Artichoke Caponata

Zingy White Beans and Tomatoes

Grape and Goat

PROSCIUTTO + FIG JAM ON TOASTED POINTS

Scallop Carpaccio with Kalamata-Orange Relish and Lemon Aioli

MAKES 12 APPETIZER-SIZE TOASTS

Carpaccio is a fancy toast. There's nothing complicated about it, but call it carpaccio and there's instant cred. The term is used for anything thinly sliced and raw, but a just-as-tasty alternative is to chop up the scallops, cure them in lemon juice for 15 to 20 minutes, and then mix in the rest of the ingredients. Then you can call it ceviche.

4 sea scallops

6 tablespoons freshly squeezed lemon juice

¾ cup finely chopped peeled orange segments (from about ½ navel orange), with 1 or 2 tablespoons orange juice from chopping reserved

¾ teaspoon salt

¼ teaspoon freshly ground black pepper

¼ cup finely chopped red onion

¼ cup finely chopped Kalamata olives

½ cup mayonnaise

1 teaspoon lemon zest

12 ¼-inch-thick baguette slices, oven-toasted (see page 8)

Parsley, for garnish

1. Thinly slice the scallops horizontally, to make 3 slices per scallop, and place them in a small bowl. Add 3 tablespoons of the lemon juice, the reserved orange juice, the salt, and pepper and set aside to marinate for 10 to 15 minutes.

2. To make the Kalamata-orange relish, in a small bowl, combine the orange, 1 tablespoon of the lemon juice, the onion, and the olives. Set aside.

3. To make the lemon aioli, in another small bowl, mix the mayonnaise, the remaining 2 tablespoons lemon juice, and the lemon zest.

4. Spread each toast with 1 tablespoon lemon aioli. Top with 1 scallop slice and 1 tablespoon Kalamata-orange relish. Garnish with parsley.

Nectarine Caprese

A reminder not to overthink things—the simplest things can wow. Cupcakes are just cake in a muffin tin, and it doesn't get much simpler than adding bacon to anything and everything. Or the concept: top it with an egg and call it brunch. Nectarines in caprese get people excited, too (which works out well because nectarines and tomatoes are seasonally compatible). This is a communal toast: the caprese sits atop a ring of baguette slices.

---

1 perfectly ripe white nectarine

1 large red tomato

1 1-pound ball fresh handmade mozzarella

1 baguette, sliced into ½-inch rounds, pan-toasted in oil (see page 6)

¼ cup loosely packed small basil leaves

¼ teaspoon salt

½ teaspoon freshly ground black pepper

Olive oil, for drizzling

---

1. Slice the nectarine, tomato, and mozzarella into ½-inch-thick round slices.

2. Arrange the toasts in a circle on a large plate and fan the components of the caprese on top.

3. Top with the basil, salt, and pepper and a drizzle of oil.

Grilled Hearts of Palm with Saffron Hummus

MAKES 12 APPETIZER-SIZE TOASTS

Grilling hearts of palm is a new-school song with an old-school ingredient, like Lou Reed collaborating with Gorillaz. Start with good ingredients and enhance them in unorthodox ways. Saffron brings a girly frill to the stage.

1 tablespoon white sesame seeds

3 tablespoons olive oil

½ large white onion, finely chopped (about 1 cup)

6 saffron threads

¼ cup white wine

1 15-ounce can white beans, rinsed and drained

2 tablespoons freshly squeezed lemon juice, plus more to taste

1 15-ounce can hearts of palm, drained

3 tablespoons aged balsamic vinegar

2 tablespoons honey

12 small 1-inch-thick slices rye bread, pan-toasted using the heavy-soaking technique (see page 6)

½ teaspoon salt

¼ teaspoon freshly ground black pepper

1. In a medium saucepan over medium-low heat, toast the sesame seeds, stirring often, 2 to 3 minutes. Transfer to a paper towel or plate to cool.

2. In the same pan over medium-low heat, add 2 tablespoons of the oil and the onion. Sauté until the onion is soft, 7 to 10 minutes, then add the saffron and sauté until the onion is very translucent and the saffron is fragrant, 2 to 3 more minutes. Add the wine and cook down until the wine is gone, 2 to 3 minutes.

3. In a blender, puree the mixture, adding the white beans and the lemon juice; process until smooth. Add more lemon juice if desired.

(continued)

4. Slice the hearts of palm on the bias and brush with the remaining 1 tablespoon oil. Heat a grill or grill pan on medium-high heat. When hot, grill until they are softened and grill marks form, 5 to 7 minutes.

5. Meanwhile, make a quick balsamic reduction with the vinegar and honey: In a small saucepan over medium heat, cook the liquids down to about 4 teaspoons.

6. Spread a layer of hummus on each toast and sprinkle on salt and pepper. Place the hearts of palm atop. Sprinkle with the sesame seeds and a drizzle of the balsamic.

Herbed Goat Cheese and Grilled Vegetables

This herby goat cheese goes well with every vegetable under the sun. Make a batch and spread the love. Double the recipe and you'll have enough for toast, plus extra cheese for a salad, to toss with red quinoa, brown rice, or scrambled eggs. Slice radishes and apples, open a can of chickpeas, and mix it all up with a few chilled cheese crumbles and a squeeze of lemon. Or save some to use with sliced avocados. It's the goat that keeps on giving.

And you'll have lots of extra herbs to go around as well—spread the love on all of the above.

6 ounces goat cheese, at room temp

2 tablespoons chopped parsley

2 tablespoons chopped cilantro

2 tablespoons chopped basil

1 tablespoon chopped oregano

1 tablespoon chopped mint

½ teaspoon ground sumac

1 teaspoon freshly ground black pepper

2 teaspoons orange zest

2 cups vegetables: halved asparagus spears, green beans, zucchini coins, and any other vegetable you see that would be good to grill

Olive oil, for grilling

8 to 12 ½-inch-thick slices baguette, cut on the bias and grilled (see page 8)

Squeeze of orange juice

U-PICK

1. In a medium bowl, mix the softened goat cheese with the parsley, cilantro, basil, oregano, mint, sumac, pepper, and orange zest.

2. Heat a grill or grill pan to medium-high heat. Toss vegetables of your choice with oil and grill until they form grill marks, 7 to 10 minutes.

(continued)

3. Spread a little less than 2 tablespoons of the goat cheese mixture evenly on each toast. Top the toasts with grilled veggies, either a single kind per toast or mix it up— you pick! Finish with a tiny squeeze of orange over all the toasts.

Sumac is a lemony-flavored spice used in a lot of Middle Eastern food. What to do once you have it in the pantry? Roast sweet potatoes and chickpeas with it and top with crème fraîche and red chiles. Add it to stews and soups.

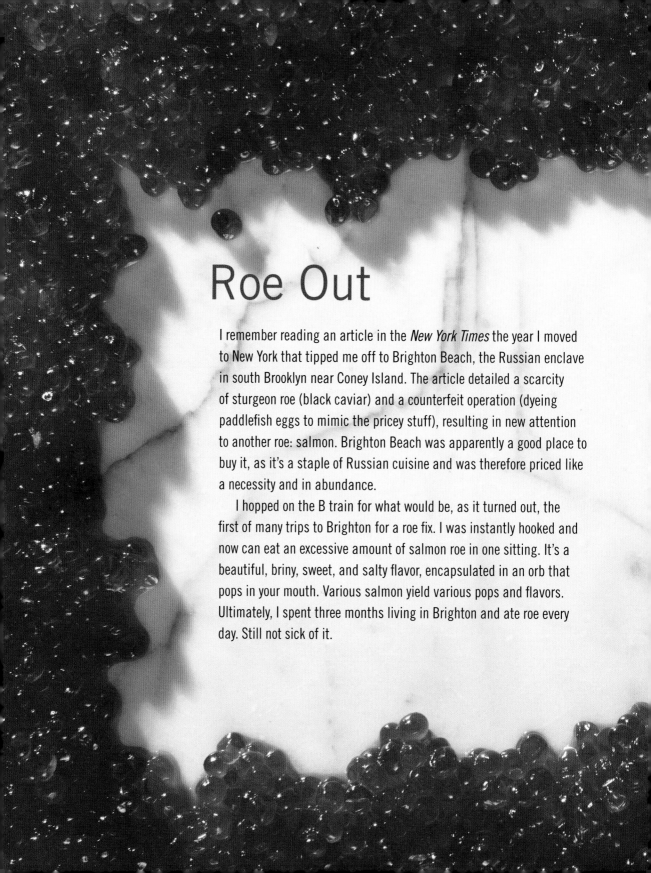

Roe Out

I remember reading an article in the *New York Times* the year I moved
to New York that tipped me off to Brighton Beach, the Russian enclave
in south Brooklyn near Coney Island. The article detailed a scarcity
of sturgeon roe (black caviar) and a counterfeit operation (dyeing
paddlefish eggs to mimic the pricey stuff), resulting in new attention
to another roe: salmon. Brighton Beach was apparently a good place to
buy it, as it's a staple of Russian cuisine and was therefore priced like
a necessity and in abundance.

I hopped on the B train for what would be, as it turned out, the
first of many trips to Brighton for a roe fix. I was instantly hooked and
now can eat an excessive amount of salmon roe in one sitting. It's a
beautiful, briny, sweet, and salty flavor, encapsulated in an orb that
pops in your mouth. Various salmon yield various pops and flavors.
Ultimately, I spent three months living in Brighton and ate roe every
day. Still not sick of it.

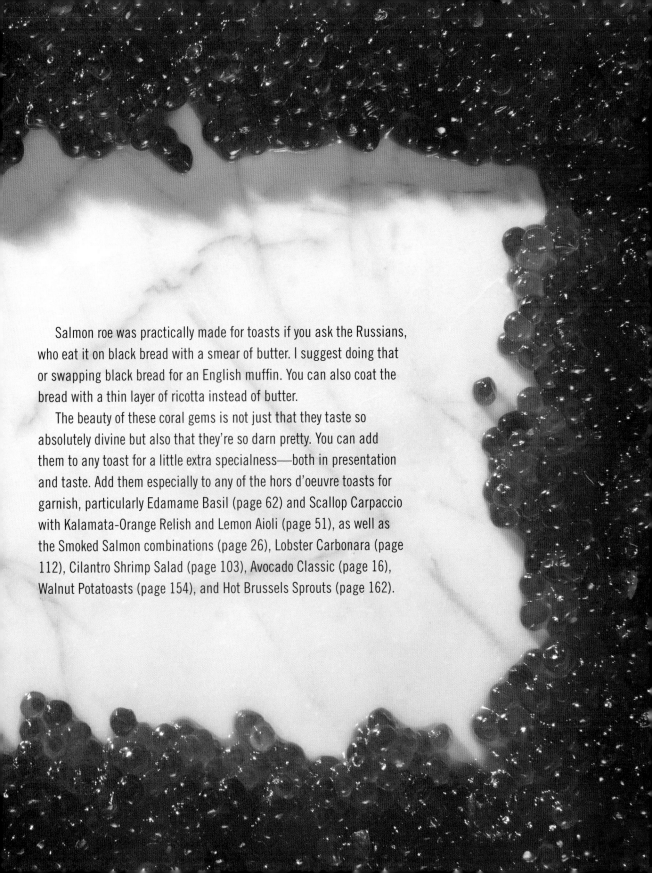

Salmon roe was practically made for toasts if you ask the Russians, who eat it on black bread with a smear of butter. I suggest doing that or swapping black bread for an English muffin. You can also coat the bread with a thin layer of ricotta instead of butter.

The beauty of these coral gems is not just that they taste so absolutely divine but also that they're so darn pretty. You can add them to any toast for a little extra specialness—both in presentation and taste. Add them especially to any of the hors d'oeuvre toasts for garnish, particularly Edamame Basil (page 62) and Scallop Carpaccio with Kalamata-Orange Relish and Lemon Aioli (page 51), as well as the Smoked Salmon combinations (page 26), Lobster Carbonara (page 112), Cilantro Shrimp Salad (page 103), Avocado Classic (page 16), Walnut Potatoasts (page 154), and Hot Brussels Sprouts (page 162).

Edamame Basil

This pretty toast is healthy and tastes like a magnificent treat. It's an awesome change of pace from hummus and works in any setting—make it delicate with edible flowers, endive, or sesame seeds or bulk it up with Seared Tuna Tatsoi (see page 76). It's an insouciant cook's neon green dream. Since the only real prep work is blending up the ingredients, the hardest part for you is choosing which flower to place on each toast.

1 12-ounce bag frozen preshelled edamame, thawed (2⅓ cups)

6 large basil leaves

½ cup olive oil

2 tablespoons rice vinegar

1 tablespoon freshly squeezed lemon juice

1 teaspoon salt

½ teaspoon freshly ground black pepper

1 sesame baguette, cut into ¼-inch-thick slices on the bias and oven-toasted with oil (see page 8)

1 endive, sliced ¼ inch thick (optional)

Edible flowers (optional)

1 tablespoon black sesame seeds (optional)

1. In a blender or food processor, puree the edamame, basil, oil, vinegar, lemon juice, salt, and pepper until supersmooth.

2. Spread 2 tablespoons of puree on each toast. Top with any combination of endive, edible flowers, or sesame seeds (if using).

Hot Miso Crab

This works as a fancy little passed hors d'oeuvre toast or as a more substantial dinner toast. As an hors d'oeuvre, it'll pair especially well with rosé but also any sparkling wine or crisp white. If you're eating it for dinner, sauté some garlicky bok choy or watercress on the side, plus a little kimchi for bite. If you're tight on cash but still want to impress, this is a great one—you don't need to buy the most expensive crab; the miso makes up for it. That said, it's always best to buy the highest quality you can afford.

½ cup silken tofu

3 tablespoons white miso

1 tablespoon freshly squeezed lemon juice

2 tablespoons sherry vinegar (or malt vinegar if that's lying around)

½ teaspoon garlic powder

1 teaspoon onion powder

¼ teaspoon cayenne

½ teaspoon freshly ground black pepper

1 8-ounce can jumbo lump crab

¼ cup sour cream

2 tablespoons finely chopped fresh chives

Olive oil

1 loaf miche bread or baguette, cut into 15 to 20 ½-inch-thick slices

1. Preheat the oven to 375°F and line a baking sheet with parchment paper.

2. With an immersion blender or a food processor, puree the tofu, miso, lemon juice, vinegar, garlic powder, onion powder, cayenne, and pepper until smooth.

3. Transfer to a small bowl and fold in the crab, sour cream, and chives.

4. Pour ¼ inch of oil into a shallow dish and soak the bread in the oil, coating both sides.

5. Evenly heap 2 to 3 tablespoons of the crab mixture onto each slice of bread and lay the slices on the prepared baking sheet. Bake for 12 to 14 minutes, until a little browned. Serve hot.

Pesto Swirl

BUST OUT THE KITCHEN SHEARS & MAKE PESTO.

Made with garlic and lots of basil, it has an intense flavor. See how easy making your own pesto is; freeze what you don't use, or eat it for breakfast the next day. I omit traditional pine nuts in this recipe because texture is covered by the ricotta, which offers a smooth, soothing, almost coy creaminess in the midst of abundant summer basil. Want to make the ricotta, too? Then use the recipes in the book (see page 130—maybe make basil ricotta and call it double-basil-pesto) and you'll have lots left over so you can eat homemade cheese for breakfast, too. If you don't make either, this will take you two seconds and still be scrumptious.

Bunch of basil (about 2 cups)

3 tablespoons olive oil

3 garlic cloves, halved

2 tablespoons grated Parmesan

1 tablespoon lemon zest

2 tablespoons freshly squeezed lemon juice

1 cup plain ricotta (see page 130)

1 sourdough baguette, cut into ½-inch-thick slices, and oven-toasted (see page 8)

1. With an immersion blender or in a regular blender, puree the basil, oil, one of the garlic cloves, the Parmesan, lemon zest, and lemon juice until smooth.

2. Transfer to a bowl and gently fold in the ricotta.

3. Rub the toast vigorously with the 2 remaining garlic cloves. Slather the ricotta mixture on top.

Kale and Artichoke Caponata

This toast is briny and acidic . . . pucker up, *mi amor*! But capers are optional if you want to tone it down. To censor it more, toss the caponata in crème fraîche or cream cheese and serve it as a dip. For extra love, set up these toasts in advance and then pop them in the oven with a thin layer of Asiago or Manchego cheese. Serve to guests hot. Serve to me however.

Bunch of lacinato kale, stemmed and coarsely chopped

¼ cup olive oil

1 celery stalk, diced (about ½ cup)

1 red onion, finely chopped (about 1 cup)

4 garlic cloves, minced

1 medium vine-ripened tomato, diced (about ½ cup)

½ cup dry white wine

¼ cup white wine vinegar

1 8-ounce jar artichoke hearts, drained and chopped

½ cup pitted green olives, chopped

1 tablespoon turbinado sugar

1 tablespoon small capers, drained (optional)

½ cup diced dried apricots

¼ cup walnuts, toasted (see page 9) and chopped

½ teaspoon freshly ground black pepper

10 ¼-inch-thick slices whole wheat sourdough bread or baguette, Parmesan pan-toasted (see page 7)

¼ cup julienned basil (optional)

Grated Parmesan, for garnish (optional)

1. In a large saucepan over medium heat, steam the kale in about 1 inch of water for 2 to 4 minutes. Remove the kale and set aside. Drain any excess water.

2. Dry the saucepan used for the kale, place it over medium heat, and add the oil. Sauté the celery, onion, and garlic until soft, 3 to 5 minutes.

3. Add the tomato, wine, vinegar, artichokes, olives, sugar, capers, and apricots. Reduce the heat to low. Simmer until everything is a bit broken down and the liquid is reduced, 12 to 15 minutes.

4. Stir in the kale, walnuts, and pepper.

5. Divide the caponata among the toasts. If desired, top with the basil shreds and a sprinkling of grated Parmesan.

Zingy White Beans and Tomatoes

MAKES 8 TO 12 APPETIZER-SIZE TOASTS

White beans and tomatoes are old-school BFFs. And they get better after hanging out for a few days once they've been cooked together. White beans are exceptionally good for you with a load of antioxidants, magnesium, and fiber, plus they are low on the glycemic index and help regulate fat storage in the body. Creamy, dense, mild, and smooth beans plus zingy, blistery tomatoes—the Felix and Oscar of toast mash-ups, respectively.

5 tablespoons olive oil

4 fresh rosemary sprigs

2 garlic cloves, chopped

1 15-ounce can white beans, rinsed and drained

Pinch of salt

1 pint cherry tomatoes, halved, or 1 15-ounce can diced tomatoes, drained

1 tablespoon sherry vinegar

1 lemon, halved

4 ½-inch-thick slices rustic Italian bread, Parmesan pan-toasted (see page 7), halved or cut in thirds to make bite-size pieces

1. In a medium saucepan over low heat, heat the oil and the rosemary sprigs until the rosemary has fried up but not burned, 5 to 7 minutes. Remove the sprigs and reserve them. Set aside 2 tablespoons of the rosemary oil (just scoop it out with a spoon and put it in a little cup).

2. Add the garlic and white beans, turn up the heat, and sauté for 4 to 6 minutes, until the garlic is softened. Add the salt.

3. Add the tomatoes and cook them down, about 10 minutes, stirring occasionally. Add the vinegar and cook another 2 minutes, until the mixture comes together.

4. Squeeze the lemon onto the toasts and top with roughly 2 tablespoons bean-tomato mix. Drizzle uniformly with the reserved rosemary oil and top with the fried rosemary.

Grape and Goat

This is a sophisticated little toast (hello, blue cheese) to serve with wine. It's an all-season kind of toast but becomes very special if you make it in the fall with Concord grapes from the farmers' market. Extra baked grapes can be used in a salad with feta the next day. Or you could mix everything together here (grapes into the cheese) and make it a grapey spread, which would be fantastic as a solo component to spread on toast but also, for a meat eater, great with leftover Thanksgiving turkey.

2 teaspoons honey

2 fresh rosemary sprigs

4 tablespoons olive oil

2 cups red grapes (¾ to 1 pound), halved

½ teaspoon balsamic vinegar

½ teaspoon salt

1 teaspoon freshly ground black pepper

1 demi-baguette, halved lengthwise and cut into 8 pieces

4 ounces goat cheese, softened

2 tablespoons blue cheese, such as Humboldt Fog

← to keep it goat

1. Preheat the oven to 425°F and line a rimmed baking sheet with parchment paper.

2. In a small pot over low heat, combine the honey, rosemary, and oil. Simmer for about 5 minutes, or until the mixture starts to smell very fragrant.

3. In a small bowl, toss the grapes with half the oil mixture, the rosemary sprigs (recycled from the oil mixture), vinegar, salt, and pepper.

4. Spread the grapes on the baking sheet and bake for 30 minutes. They should be desiccated a bit but not dried up (reserve any juices left on the baking sheet).

5. Meanwhile, heat a grill or grill pan over high heat and grill the bread with the remainder of the honey-oil (see page 8).

6. Mix the cheeses together and spread them on the grilled bread.

7. Top the toasts with the grapes and juices from the baking sheet. Discard the rosemary sprigs.

4 non-veg toasts

Seared Tuna Tatsoi

Escargots and Mushrooms

Niçoise

Marinated Shrimp, Celery, and Green Olives

Fig Bagna Cauda and Watercress

Chickpea and Chorizo

Thai Crab and Cucumber

Paprika Sherry Shrimp Skillet

Chile-Orange-Cured Salmon with Cilantro Crème Fraîche

Rosemary Caper Tuna Salad

Bay Scallops and Pear-Onion Jam

Grandpa Sardines

Cilantro Shrimp Salad

French Onion Toast

Fresh Sardines and Parsley-Apricot Gremolata

Grilled Zucchini and Bottarga

Lobster Carbonara

- LOBSTER + MAYO + LEMON ZEST + CHIVES

Seared Tuna Tatsoi

It's as if Lilly Pulitzer were an Asian toast. All that pink and green. The tuna, that oh-so-girly radish, and such delicate lettuce make a ladylike tripling. Tatsoi has an almost creamy taste that envelops the radish, while melt-in-your-mouth tuna gets a boost from sesame and soy. If you're looking to add a little sass, mix in some wasabi with the dressing in step 2.

1 pound ahi tuna, rinsed and patted dry

1 tablespoon olive oil

1 tablespoon plus ½ teaspoon sesame oil

2 tablespoons rice vinegar

2 tablespoons soy sauce

1 to 3 watermelon radishes (about 1 cup sliced)

¾ cup tatsoi or another subtle green, such as baby spinach, loosely packed

1 tablespoon freshly ground black pepper (less if you're not a pepper fiend)

⅓ cup mayonnaise

12 ¼-inch-thick slices whole wheat baguette

3 scallions (white and light green parts), chopped

Black sesame seeds

WATERMELON RADISH ON A MANDOLINE

1. Cut the tuna into 3 even pieces. Heat the olive oil in a medium saucepan over medium heat, add the tuna, and sear each side, 45 seconds to 1½ minutes, to yield a rare center and an ever-so-slightly-seared crust. Let cool. Slice into ½-inch pieces.

2. In a medium bowl, combine 1 tablespoon of the sesame oil, the vinegar, and the soy sauce. Add the tuna to the bowl and toss with the dressing. Set aside.

3. Slice the radishes very thin using a mandoline or a very sharp knife. Mix them in with the tuna along with the tatsoi.

4. In a small bowl, combine the pepper, mayonnaise, and the remaining ½ teaspoon sesame oil. Spread the seasoned mayo evenly on both sides of the bread slices and pan-toast using the method on page 7.

5. Top each toast with the tuna salad. Sprinkle with the scallions and sesame seeds.

Escargots and Mushrooms

(Muscartoast? Escarshroom?)

My friend Erin (food stylist! chef! Roller Derby queen!) made a toast similar to this and most people didn't realize they were eating escargots. Not that it would have mattered—we were a foodie crew—but there's a stigma to snails. Unfair! Pair them with button mushrooms, cook them in wine, and then snails become seductive. If you have rosemary and thyme—fresh or even dried—add them to the recipe and make it an herb party.

2 shallots, chopped

2 garlic cloves, chopped

2½ tablespoons olive oil

2 pints white button mushrooms, quartered

1 8-ounce can escargots, rinsed and patted dry

½ cup white wine

1 cup chopped parsley, plus more for garnish

½ teaspoon salt

¼ teaspoon freshly ground black pepper

2 tablespoons (¼ stick) unsalted butter, softened

½ cup grated Parmesan

8 ¼-inch-thick slices baguette

1. Preheat the oven to 350°F.

2. In a medium pan over medium heat, sauté the shallots and the garlic in 2 tablespoons of the oil until softened, 3 to 5 minutes.

(*continued*)

3. Add the mushrooms and escargots with the remaining ½ tablespoon oil and sauté another 5 minutes, or until the escargots are firmed up and the mushrooms are softened all the way through.

4. Add the wine and let it cook off completely, 3 to 5 minutes.

5. Turn off the heat and stir in 1 cup of the parsley, the salt, and pepper (and other herbs, too, if you have them).

6. Mix the butter, any herbs you have in the house (e.g., rosemary, thyme, etc.), and Parmesan and spread the mixture evenly on the bread. Lay the bread on a baking sheet and toast in the oven until melty and golden brown, about 10 minutes.

7. Top the toasts with the mushroom-escargot mixture. Garnish with more parsley and serve immediately.

Niçoise

I can't stop eating anchovies packed with omega-3s, B vitamins, calcium, and iron (see page 87). Niçoise is merely another vehicle, which is why this one is a you-decide-your-own-level-of-involvement toast platter. So long as I get lots of anchovies, you get lots of what you want. We're a match made in heaven.

8 small Yukon Gold potatoes, scrubbed

12 ounces fresh green beans, trimmed

3 large eggs

2 sun-dried tomatoes

1 teaspoon capers, drained

2 tablespoons lemon juice

3 tablespoons olive oil

2 yellow bell peppers, roasted (see page 83), cored, seeded, and sliced

2 cans good-quality tuna, drained and broken into pieces

3 tablespoons pitted, chopped Niçoise or Kalamata olives

4 jarred anchovies, such as Ortiz brand

4 demi-baguettes, halved lengthwise, then cut into two crosswise, oven-toasted with oil (see page 8)

1. Bring a large pot of heavily salted water to a boil over high heat. Add the potatoes and cook until soft, 15 to 20 minutes. Drain, cool, and slice ¼ inch thick. Set on a large platter.

2. Meanwhile, in a separate pot of water, blanch the green beans. Remove with a slotted spoon and slice in thirds crosswise. Set on the platter.

3. For ease, in the same pot of water from the green beans, hard-boil the eggs (see page 38 for the best method), cool, peel, and slice ¼ inch thick. Set on the platter.

4. While the eggs are boiling, chop the sun-dried tomatoes and capers together on a cutting board until they become a paste. Transfer them to a small bowl and mix in the lemon juice and oil. Set on the platter.

(continued)

5. To the platter, add the peppers, tuna, and olives. Place the anchovies in a small bowl to accompany the platter.

6. Arrange the toasts around the platter on the table or in a bowl and invite everyone to top them as desired.

ROASTING PEPPERS

To roast a bell pepper on a gas stove, turn it to medium-high heat and put the pepper (whole) on the burner directly over the flame. Let it blacken, turning it carefully with tongs to reach all the skin. Let cool, then peel off and discard the skin. If roasting in the oven, seed and slice peppers in quarters. Toss them in 1 tablespoon olive oil and spread evenly on a parchment-lined baking sheet. Broil the peppers for 15 to 20 minutes, until the skin of the peppers is blackened in spots. You can peel the skin if you don't want that char or eat it if you like it.

If that doesn't sound like something you have time for today, don't feel guilty about buying peppers preroasted from the store.

Marinated Shrimp, Celery, and Green Olives

MAKES 10 TOASTS, WITH SOME LEFTOVER TOPPING

I am thinking about the weekend. Thinking about a picnic: at the beach? in a park? in a parking lot? Doesn't really matter where a weekend pit stop happens as long as you're prepared. This salad works well because it gets better as it marinates and provides plenty to share. Aces.

3 tablespoons sugar

3 tablespoons salt

3 bay leaves

12 to 15 shrimp (about 10 ounces U21/25), peeled and deveined

1 15-ounce can hearts of palm, drained and sliced

2 to 3 celery stalks, sliced 1/8 inch thick on the bias (about 1½ cups)—a mandoline works best

½ cup torn parsley leaves

½ cup Castelvetrano olives (or another hearty green olive), pitted and chopped

¼ cup Marcona almonds or blanched, salted almonds

½ cup quartered, sliced Vidalia onion

¼ cup freshly squeezed lemon juice

3 tablespoons almond or olive oil

10 ¼-inch-thick slices whole wheat sourdough bread, pan-toasted using the heavy-soaking technique (see page 6)

1. Bring a medium pot of water to a boil over high heat with the sugar, salt, and bay leaves and boil, covered, for 10 minutes. Add the shrimp and boil until opaque, 4 to 6 minutes. Drain the shrimp and set them aside to cool (rinse them under cold water if you're short on time).

2. Meanwhile, in a large bowl, combine the hearts of palm, celery, parsley, olives, almonds, onion, lemon juice, and oil.

3. Slice each shrimp into 2 or 3 thin pieces, lengthwise, and then into 2 or 3 pieces across. Mix with the rest of the salad, cover, and refrigerate for 20 minutes or more.

4. Top the toasts with the chilled shrimp salad.

Fig Bagna Cauda and Watercress

I'm an anchovy fiend (more on that on page 81), and bagna cauda is a liquid Italian delivery system for them: traditionally a hot, thin dip composed of my favorite little fishies, garlic, butter, and olive oil. I make it into a spread and add a few of my other favorite ingredients. But, you! Don't skimp on the 'chovies. Give them a try. They perk up your taste buds to the flavors of everything else. This spread can be made in advance and lasts in the fridge for a handful of days. It's one of my favorite recipes in the book.

8 dried figs

1 tablespoon capers, drained

1 garlic clove

10 mint leaves

5 anchovy fillets

1 cup pitted Kalamata olives

4 ounces goat cheese, softened

½ teaspoon freshly ground black pepper

Bunch of watercress, stems trimmed (about 2 cups)

⅓ cup chopped walnuts

3 tablespoons freshly squeezed lemon juice

10 ¼-inch-thick slices dark rye, pumpernickel, or Quinoa-Millet Bread (see page 11)

1. Preheat the oven to 350°F.

2. In a blender, puree the figs, capers, garlic, mint, anchovies, and olives (a little liquid from the olive jar isn't bad).

3. Transfer the paste to a small bowl and mix in the goat cheese and pepper.

4. In another small bowl, mix the watercress, walnuts, and lemon juice.

5. Spread the fig bagna cauda evenly on the bread slices and spread them out on a rimmed baking sheet. Warm them in the oven for 8 to 10 minutes, or until the spread is a little baked.

6. Pile some watercress salad on top of each toast and serve.

Chickpea and Chorizo

This is a dinnertime toast. It looks gorgeous and can be #eatenwithaforkandknife. Avocado acts as the creamy agent here, but you could also pan-toast your bread in oil or mayonnaise (see pages 6 and 7) and omit the avo. Puncturing cherry tomatoes releases their luscious juices, heightening the flavors of the dish. Serve with a green salad and call everyone to the table.

2 shallots, chopped (about ½ cup)

2 tablespoons olive oil

½ pound fresh chorizo, thinly sliced

1 cup cherry tomatoes, punctured

3 tablespoons tomato paste

½ teaspoon freshly ground black pepper

½ teaspoon red chili pepper flakes

½ 15-ounce can chickpeas, rinsed and drained

½ cup white wine

1 teaspoon sherry vinegar (optional)

1 ripe avocado, pitted and peeled

6 ½-inch-thick slices sourdough rye bread, toasted using the plain-old-toast technique (see page 8)

2 tablespoons freshly squeezed lemon juice

½ teaspoon salt

2 tablespoons chopped parsley

2 tablespoons chopped cilantro

1. In a large pan over medium heat, sauté the shallots in the oil until soft, about 5 minutes. Add the chorizo and sauté another 1 to 2 minutes. Add the tomatoes and let them soften, releasing their juices, about 5 minutes.

2. Add the tomato paste to thicken along with the pepper and chili flakes. Mix to incorporate, then add the chickpeas, wine, and vinegar (if using) and simmer to reduce until the liquid is gone.

3. Smash the avocado into the toasts and sprinkle with lemon juice and salt.

4. Top the toasts with the chorizo and chickpea mixture and the parsley and cilantro.

Plan this ahead! You can make the chorizo-chickpea mixture up to 2 days in advance.

Thai Crab and Cucumber

This is a dreamy toast, drawing inspiration from time spent eating my way through Southeast Asia with my mother. Citrus and fish sauce are balanced by coconut and cucumber. Keep the chiles in the oil if you need a wake-up call. I use cucumbers in two preparations in this recipe; but you won't need more than one Kirby in total (or half of a medium regular cuke).

---

3 tablespoons coconut oil

2 garlic cloves, smashed

1 serrano chile pepper, cored, seeded, and finely chopped

½ cup chopped Kirby cucumber*

⅓ cup finely diced red onion

2 tablespoons finely chopped cilantro

2 tablespoons finely chopped mint

2 tablespoons freshly squeezed lemon juice

3 tablespoons freshly squeezed lime juice

¼ teaspoon fish sauce (optional)

6 ounces jumbo lump crab

6 ¼-inch-thick slices soft white bread, such as brioche, baguette, ciabatta, or similar

½ cup thinly sliced Kirby cucumber*

---

1. Preheat the oven to 350°F.

2. In a small saucepan over low heat, blend the oil, garlic, and chile. Let the oil heat until the garlic starts to sizzle. Turn off the heat and discard the garlic and chile. Transfer the oil to a small bowl.

3. In a medium bowl, combine the chopped cucumber, onion, cilantro, mint, lemon juice, lime juice, and fish sauce (if using). Mix in the crab and 2 tablespoons of the infused oil.

4. Brush the remaining 1 tablespoon infused oil onto the bread and oven-toast the bread (see page 8), about 10 minutes.

5. Lay the cucumber slices on the toasts and top each one with about 3 tablespoons of the crab mixture.

*If you can't find Kirby cukes, get English cukes instead. Regular ones are fine, too. Use a mandoline to make the cucumber slices if you have one.

Paprika Sherry Shrimp Skillet

Serving dinner from the skillet means built-in warming capabilities, pretty presentation, and one less dish to do. You're winning. Not that it's a competition.

3 tablespoons olive oil

¼ cup sherry vinegar, plus more for finishing

2 garlic cloves, minced

1 bay leaf

½ teaspoon paprika, plus more for garnish

½ pound shrimp (U21/25), peeled and deveined

3 strips lemon rind

2 tablespoons lemon juice

6 ¼-inch-thick slices miche bread or another round, light sourdough bread, oven-toasted with oil (see page 8) and made extra crispy

1. In a medium bowl, mix together the oil, ¼ cup of the vinegar, the garlic, bay leaf, and paprika. Add the shrimp, cover, and refrigerate for 30 minutes to let marinate.

2. Preheat a skillet over medium-high heat and add the shrimp (including the marinade). Add the lemon rind and lemon juice and sauté until the shrimp are opaque, 5 to 6 minutes.

3. Garnish with a splash of sherry vinegar and a sprinkling of paprika.

4. Serve the shrimp from the skillet with the toast on the side.

Chile-Orange-Cured Salmon with Cilantro Crème Fraîche

MAKES 6 TOASTS*

Cured salmon is the little sister to smoked salmon. A little gentler, a little wilder, and definitely without a curfew—she's good any time of day. Tell the fishmonger you're curing salmon so that he takes extra care to remove all the pin bones and does a good job filleting.

2 tablespoons chili powder

¼ cup sugar

⅓ cup kosher salt

Freshly ground black pepper

3 tablespoons orange zest (from about 1 medium orange)

1 1-pound salmon fillet, skin removed

½ cup cilantro, roughly chopped

1 tablespoon freshly squeezed orange juice

1 tablespoon freshly squeezed lemon juice

½ cup crème fraîche (or sour cream)

6 ¼-inch-thick slices whole wheat sourdough or rye bread, toasted using the plain-old-toast technique (see page 8)

1. In a small bowl, mix together the chili powder, sugar, salt, 1 teaspoon pepper, and the orange zest, pinching the mixture with your fingers to release the oils from the zest.

2. Rub the mixture evenly all over the salmon. Using a couple feet of plastic wrap, wrap the salmon tightly but not supertight, because the salt needs a little room to cure the fish.

3. Place the wrapped fish on a plate and place another plate on top of it. Place this setup in the fridge and set some heavy things on top of it to put pressure on the salmon.

*There will be lots of leftover salmon (good for another week in the fridge) and crème. (See page 26 about smoked salmon and use your cured salmon to make a few of those easy combos.)

4. After 4 days, remove the fish. Rinse thoroughly. Pat dry and slice as thin as possible. You can leave it for a day or so longer if you want it more cured (firmer and more flavorful).

5. Using an immersion blender, mix the cilantro with the orange and lemon juices. Fold in the crème fraîche.

6. Spread about 2 tablespoons of the crème mixture on each toast and top with a few slices of salmon and some pepper.

Rosemary Caper Tuna Salad

MAKES 12 TOASTS

Maison Kayser's epi baguette makes for a synesthetic experience, and Bouchon Bakery has an equally euphoric epi. If you ask your local baker to make one for you, he may just do it. It's an inspiring piece of dough: baguette ingredients in the shape of leaves, made to pull apart at the table—an epi encourages communal camaraderie.

½ cup olive oil

6 fresh rosemary sprigs

4 4-ounce cans tuna packed in water (or oil if you are using imported), drained

4 tablespoons mayonnaise

2 teaspoons grainy mustard

4 tablespoons lemon zest

6 tablespoons freshly squeezed lemon juice

2 to 3 Kirby cucumbers, or ½ English cucumber, diced (1 to 1½ cups)

2 to 3 celery stalks, diced (1 to 2 cups)

½ cup chopped parsley

¼ cup small capers, drained and patted dry

1 epi baguette, sliced across, oven-toasted dry (see page 8)

12 Bibb lettuce leaves

1. In a medium saucepan over low heat, heat the oil and the rosemary sprigs until the rosemary has fried up but not burned, 5 to 7 minutes. Remove the sprigs. Pour the oil into a small bowl and let cool.

2. In a medium bowl, mix the tuna, mayonnaise, mustard, lemon zest, and lemon juice until combined. Mix in ¼ cup of the rosemary oil, the cucumbers, celery, and parsley.

3. In a medium skillet over medium-high heat, heat 2 tablespoons of the rosemary oil and fry the capers until crisped up, about 3 minutes. Let cool on a paper towel.

4. Keeping the epi "leaves" connected on each bread half, assemble the toasts by topping each epi "leaf" with a drizzle of the remaining 2 tablespoons rosemary oil. Top each with a Bibb lettuce leaf, a scoop of tuna salad, and some fried capers. Bring to the table whole and let your guests break off a bread "leaf" to serve themselves.

Bay Scallops and Pear-Onion Jam

Bay scallops are an extrasweet treat from the sea. Capitalize on them when the season hits by marrying them to pears and onions; just remember the black pepper for balance. The hearty flavors are bolstered by grilling the bread (and the scallops). So if you have access to a grill (or grill pan), bust it out.

2 cups chopped white onion

3 tablespoons olive oil, plus more for pan-toasting the bread

1 tablespoon apple cider vinegar

1 Bartlett pear, cored and chopped (about 1¼ cups)

½ cup turbinado sugar

Freshly ground black pepper

1 tablespoon chopped rosemary

½ cup balsamic vinegar

2 fresh rosemary sprigs

30 bay scallops (or 10 sea scallops, cut into thirds, if you can't find bay)

6 ½-inch-thick slices rye or rustic sourdough bread

1. In a medium pan over medium heat, sauté the onion in 3 tablespoons of the oil until caramelized, 15 to 20 minutes. Deglaze the pan with the apple cider vinegar.

2. Add the pear, ¼ cup of the sugar, 1 teaspoon of the pepper, and the chopped rosemary plus water to cover (about ¼ cup) and simmer for 20 minutes, or until the pear has softened. Transfer the mixture to a bowl, mash it up but keep it a bit chunky.

3. In a small saucepan over medium-low heat, heat the balsamic vinegar, remaining ¼ cup sugar, and the rosemary sprigs. Simmer until the vinegar is reduced to about 3 tablespoons, 5 to 10 minutes. Discard the rosemary sprigs.

4. Wipe out the medium pan and sear the scallops over medium-high heat, 45 seconds to 1 minute. Cool and chop them in half if they're a little big.

5. Using the same pan for ease, pan-toast the bread using the heavy-soaking technique on page 6.

6. Spread the pear-onion jam on the toasts and top with the scallops. Drizzle with the rosemary balsamic. Sprinkle with pepper.

Grandpa Sardines

A sardine toast is only as good as the sardines you purchase. This is not a place to skimp. My grandfather loved canned sardines. He was certainly of the era during which canned sardines were a very regular pantry item. They may not be in style now, but trends are cyclical and grandfathers are always right.

¼ cup olive oil

1 cup chopped cilantro

1 garlic clove

2 tablespoons freshly squeezed lemon juice

½ teaspoon red chili flakes

4 ½-inch-thick slices soft grainy whole wheat bread, pan-toasted (see page 6)

1 4-ounce tin good-quality sardines packed in oil

1 tablespoon lemon zest

1. In a food processor or with an immersion blender, pulse the oil, cilantro, garlic, lemon juice, and chili flakes to a thick puree.

2. Spread the cilantro sauce evenly on the toasts and top them with sardines, smashing them into the toasts. Dust with lemon zest and serve.

EXTRA SARDINES? OFFLOAD THEM WITH RAISINS, PINE NUTS, AND CHOPPED BROCCOLI RABE IN BOWTIE PASTA WITH PECORINO. YUM.

Cilantro Shrimp Salad

This creamy avocado deal can be used as a sauce, a spread, a dip, and a dressing. It's many of my favorite components of a possible toast experience. If you want a little spiciness, add a serrano to the avo-yogurt.

2 tablespoons plus 1 teaspoon salt

2 tablespoons sugar

2 bay leaves

1 pound medium shrimp (U21/25), peeled and deveined

1 cup chopped cilantro, plus more for garnish

¼ cup freshly squeezed lime juice

3 tablespoons olive oil

1 ripe avocado, pitted and peeled

⅓ cup plain yogurt

12 to 14 Bibb lettuce leaves

8 ½-inch-thick slices grainy bread, pan-toasted in oil (see page 6)

1. Bring a medium pot of water, 2 tablespoons of the salt, the sugar, and bay leaves to a boil over high heat. Cover and boil for 10 minutes. Add the shrimp and boil until opaque, 4 to 6 minutes. Drain and let cool (submerge the shrimp in an ice-water bath if you're short on time).

2. Using an immersion blender or a food processor, puree 1 cup of the cilantro, the lime juice, oil, and remaining 1 teaspoon salt until smooth. Add the avocado and pulse until incorporated. Fold in the yogurt until you have a smooth mixture. ← DROOL!

3. When the shrimp are cool, slice them in half lengthwise and cut them into 1-inch pieces. Toss the shrimp in the avocado-yogurt sauce.

4. Lay 1 or 2 pieces of lettuce on each toast and add a scoop of shrimp salad to top. Garnish with extra cilantro.

French Onion Toast

I never thought about making a savory French toast until I was dazed in the back of a cab trying to find the phone number of my deli to place an order for something that would silence the demons in my stomach. As I was scrolling through my contacts, my driver stopped short, launching me and my phone into the plastic divider, forcing me to face my surroundings, which, as we made our way downtown, included a twenty-four-hour French bistro. Annoyed at the driver, not in a state to make rational decisions, and hangry, I fled the cab and went to the café. French onion soup called my name, and with the first bite, I had a stony revelation that held up the next day when I revisited my napkin scrawl.

4 tablespoons (½ stick) unsalted butter

2 or 3 large white onions, quartered and sliced (about 6 cups)

1 teaspoon salt

½ teaspoon freshly ground black pepper

1 cup half-and-half

3 large eggs

½ cup beef broth

¼ teaspoon Worcestershire sauce

½ teaspoon onion powder

Pinch of nutmeg (optional)

8 1½-inch-thick slices stale, sturdy baguette

8 slices Gruyère

3 cups spicy greens, such as mustard greens or arugula

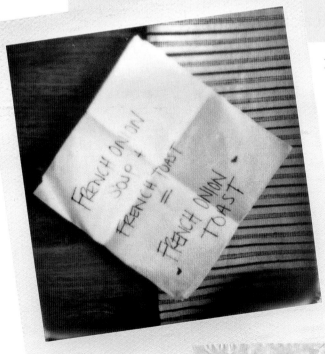

1. Preheat the oven to 375°F and line a baking sheet with parchment paper.

2. In a medium pan over low heat, heat 2 tablespoons of the butter and sauté the onions with the salt and pepper until caramelized, 30 to 40 minutes. Set aside.

3. In a medium bowl, whisk together the half-and-half, eggs, broth, Worcestershire sauce, onion powder, and nutmeg (if using).

(continued)

4. Dip each slice of bread into the liquid (about 2 seconds), letting it soak up the mixture. Set the bread slices on a platter to rest for about 1 minute.

5. In a medium pan over medium heat, melt 1 tablespoon butter. Add the soaked bread, working in batches and taking care not to crowd the pan. Let one side cook until golden and firm, 2 to 4 minutes, and then flip and cook the other side. Repeat to make the rest of the toasts, refreshing with the remaining 1 tablespoon butter.

6. Place the toasts on the prepared baking sheet. Top each with a pile of caramelized onions and a slice of Gruyère and bake for 5 to 8 minutes, or until the cheese is melty.

7. Serve hot with the spicy greens.

Fresh Sardines and Parsley-Apricot Gremolata

This recipe has a few components. It doesn't make it harder to prepare, just more of a complete meal. A tip for pitting olives? Dump the olives onto a cutting board and press a few at a time beneath the side of a large knife, gently rolling the knife back and forth until the pit is revealed. Then you should be able to remove it easily.

FENNEL SALAD
1 fennel bulb

½ cup Castelvetrano or hearty green olives, pitted and chopped

¼ cup chopped mint

2 tablespoons freshly squeezed lemon juice

GREMOLATA
½ cup chopped parsley

3 dried apricots, chopped

3 garlic cloves

2 tablespoons fresh oregano leaves

1 tablespoon lemon zest

2 tablespoons freshly squeezed lemon juice

2 tablespoons champagne vinegar

2 tablespoons olive oil

SARDINE TOASTS
6 fresh sardines, cleaned, scaled, gutted, and filleted (ask the fishmonger to do this)

½ teaspoon salt

½ teaspoon freshly ground black pepper

2 tablespoons olive oil

12 ½-inch-thick slices ciabatta, cut on the bias to accommodate the sardine shape

24 paper-thin lemon slices

1. Preheat the oven to 375°F and line a baking sheet with parchment paper.

2. Make the fennel salad: In a bowl, shave the fennel using a mandoline at its thinnest setting (⅛ inch). Mix in the olives, mint, and lemon juice and set aside.

(continued)

3. Make the gremolata: Using an immersion blender, mix the parsley, apricots, garlic, oregano, lemon zest, lemon juice, vinegar, and oil until nearly smooth. Set aside.

4. Make the sardines: Cut the sardines in half lengthwise and sprinkle them with salt and pepper. In a medium skillet over medium heat, heat the oil. Add the sardines to the pan and cook for 3 to 5 minutes per side, until crispy.

5. Spread the gremolata on the bread and top each slice with 1 sardine half. Place the lemon slices on top of the fish. Arrange the bread slices on the prepared baking sheet and bake for 10 to 12 minutes, or until the sardines are cooked through and the lemons have seized up a bit.

6. Top the toasts with the fennel salad or serve it on the side.

PITTING ADVICE

Grilled Zucchini and Bottarga

Bottarga comes in two lobes that make up the roe sac of gray mullet. The roe are tiny, golden eggs that are held by a thin casing. The sac is salted, pressed, and dried before coming to a market near you. Grilling it is a Japanese technique. If your bottarga comes in wax, remove the wax, but try not to puncture the actual natural casing of the roe—it's a little membrane layer. If your bottarga does not come waxed, proceed with the recipe as follows. Its taste is a cross between anchovies and salmon roe—salty and briny yet smooth and round. Find another use for bottarga on page 28.

8 ¼-inch-thick slices ciabatta

Olive oil

2 cups grated Parmesan

2 zucchini, halved widthwise

2 to 3 ounces whole bottarga

1 or 2 celery stalks, cut into thin half-moons

1 teaspoon lemon zest

1 tablespoon freshly squeezed lemon juice

1. Brush the bread with oil and place on a hot grill or a grill pan heated over medium-high heat. Grill until marks form, then flip. Turn the temperature down to medium and sprinkle the Parmesan evenly on top of the grilled bread. Keep on the heat until the cheese melts. Set the toasts aside.

2. Brush zucchini with olive oil and grill the zucchini and the entire chunk of bottarga until grill marks form, 7 to 10 minutes, turning them once to hit both sides. Cut the zucchini into ½-inch-thick half-moons.

3. In a medium bowl, toss the zucchini and celery with 1 tablespoon oil, the lemon zest, and lemon juice.

4. Top the toasts with the lemony vegetables.

5. Thinly slice the grilled bottarga and use it to top the toasts.

Lobster Carbonara

You've got the building blocks to luxury in this recipe. The foundations of a classic carbonara plus a little lobster meat imagined as a toast can LEGO into many forms. The chive butter will come in handy (there's extra) for grilling any seafood, not to mention serving with corn and boiled potatoes. The carbonara topping can be made a touch looser and tossed with orrechiette. And, because you can't buy just 3 ounces of lobster, you'll be picking at sweet, briny, divine leftover tail and claw. Slather a slice of bread with mayo, top with the meat, and sprinkle with chives and lemon zest (à la page 74).

½ cup roughly chopped chives, plus a few for garnish

3 tablespoons grated Parmesan

4 tablespoons (½ stick) unsalted butter, melted

8 ½-inch-thick slices soft ciabatta or brioche

4 ounces pancetta, chopped

1 garlic clove, minced

1 cup finely chopped white onion

½ cup crème fraîche

1 large egg

1 large egg yolk

½ cup grated pecorino

½ teaspoon freshly ground black pepper

3 ounces cooked lobster, cut into ½-inch dice

1. Preheat the oven to 350°F.

2. Blend the chives, Parmesan, and butter in a blender or a food processor. Spread the cheesy chive butter evenly on the bread and lay the bread on a baking sheet. Toast the bread in the oven for 8 to 10 minutes, or until golden brown. Set aside.

3. Meanwhile, in a medium pan over medium-low heat, cook the pancetta until the fat melts, about 3 minutes. Add the garlic and onion and sauté until soft, 5 to 7 minutes.

4. Turn down the heat, add the crème fraîche, and bring to a simmer.

5. In a small bowl, beat the egg and the egg yolk with the pecorino and pepper. Add it to the pan and stir to incorporate, 1 to 2 minutes. Finally, add the lobster and heat it through. Mound on each toast, garnish with chives, and eat while hot.

5 veg toasts

A Love Story: Burrata + Toast

Grilled Radicchio and Apples

Spice Roasted Radishes and Mint Feta Yogurt

Grilled Cheese with Romaine and Bosc Pear

Spinach and Sweet Pea

Big Tomato

Carrot Ribbons

Ricotta Part II: More Flavors

Golden Beets and Vadouvan Yogurt

Fennel Parmesan Slaw

Shaved Asparagus and Serrano-Basil Butter

White Bean Avo

Mushroom Hunks

Roots

Cucumber Tzatziki and Roasted Jalapeños

Delicata Squash and Orange Butter

Carrot Butter and Halloumi

Chipotle Eggplant

Cauliflower Melts

Walnut Potatoasts

Brown Sugar Chipotle Sweet Potato and Carrot

Butternut Squash, Robiola, and Apples

Roasted Eggplant and Raisin Chutney

Hot Brussels Sprouts

Spicy Red Lentil

Spiced Apple Chutney

- SLICED RADISHES + BUTTER + FLAKY SALT

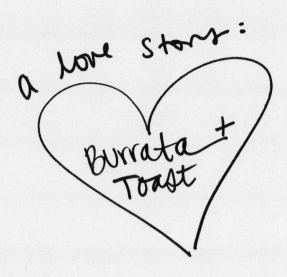

a love story: Burrata + Toast

Let's talk about burrata. Attention must be paid.

 Half solid, half liquid, it's melty and spready and presents well. And all of that goodness comes to you *just like that.* It's the cheese equivalent of a tomato. You don't have to do a thing except slide it onto the center of a plate and throw a knife in it. Putting it on a toast is extra credit. Drizzling olive oil or salt or cracking pepper is extra strength. Coupling it with Fig Bagna Cauda and Watercress (page 87) is extra lives.

 If you feel like you're slacking with just burrata, see a few adds on the opposite page:

You don't have to buy tapenade or romesco at the store. Make them yourself:
Blend up a jar of roasted red peppers with a few tablespoons of toasted pine nuts for a quick romesco.
Blend good olive oil with pitted Kalamatas for a tapenade.

ROMESCO *

A FEW BLISTERY CHERRY TOMATOES

OLIVE TAPENADE

ALWAYS TRUSTY SMASHED AVOCADO *

Grilled Radicchio and Apples

What to do when you want to make something light but can't bear the thought of another lonely night with a salad at the dinner table? Nobody puts radicchio in a corner. Grilling just might be your ticket to the dance floor.

Head of radicchio

Olive oil, for grilling

1 apple, preferably Pink Lady or Granny Smith

¼ cup chopped chives, or more to taste

1 tablespoon freshly squeezed lemon juice

1 garlic clove, grated

1 tablespoon apple cider vinegar

1 tablespoon honey

¼ cup sour cream

3 tablespoons mayonnaise

3 tablespoons buttermilk

¼ teaspoon onion powder

½ teaspoon salt

½ teaspoon freshly ground black pepper

6 ¼-inch-thick slices whole wheat bread, pan-toasted (see page 6) or grilled (see page 8)

1. Cut the radicchio into quarters. Heat a grill or grill pan over high heat. Brush the radicchio with oil and grill until softened, about 4 minutes. Then chop the radicchio.

2. Core the apple, slice it thinly, and cut the slices into matchsticks. Mix with the chives and lemon juice in a medium bowl. Set aside.

3. Make the dressing: In a medium bowl, whisk together the garlic, vinegar, honey, sour cream, mayonnaise, buttermilk, onion powder, salt, and pepper.

4. Place about ⅓ cup chopped radicchio on each toast and drizzle with the dressing. Top with the apple matchsticks. Serve immediately.

YOU'LL HAVE EXTRA DRESSING TO ADD TO SALADS OR USE AS A DIP FOR CARROTS.

Spice Roasted Radishes and Mint Feta Yogurt

Radishes-on-toast is as classic as it gets, but here's a radish revamp: roast them up, toss with fragrant spices, and pair with an herbal sauce.

2 tablespoons pine nuts

¼ teaspoon ground cinnamon

½ teaspoon ground cumin

½ teaspoon ground coriander

1 teaspoon salt

½ teaspoon freshly ground pepper

3 tablespoons olive oil, plus more for drizzling

Bunch of radishes (8 to 10)

⅓ cup feta, preferably sheep's milk

½ cup plain yogurt

10 mint leaves, roughly chopped (about 2 tablespoons)

½ teaspoon red chili pepper flakes

1 teaspoon honey

1 tablespoon lemon zest

1 tablespoon lemon juice

6 ½-inch-thick slices whole wheat bread, oven-toasted with oil (see page 8)

1. Preheat the oven to 400°F and line a baking sheet with parchment paper.

2. In a small dry pan over medium-high heat, toast the pine nuts, 3 to 5 minutes. Transfer to a dish to cool.

3. In a medium bowl, combine the cinnamon, cumin, coriander, ½ teaspoon of the salt, the pepper, and 3 tablespoons oil.

4. Wash, stem, dry, and quarter the radishes. Toss them in the spice oil to coat.

5. Spread the radishes evenly on the prepared baking sheet. Roast for 15 to 18 minutes, until soft.

6. Meanwhile, blend the feta, yogurt, mint, chili flakes, honey, lemon zest, and remaining ½ teaspoon salt.

7. Assemble the toasts by drizzling them with the minty yogurt, topping them with the radishes, and sprinkling on the lemon juice and toasted pine nuts.

Grilled Cheese with Romaine and Bosc Pear

There's the comfort-food grilled orange cheese you ate with tomato soup when you were a little girl and then there's the *moody fall day in France* version: a little more sultry; curled up in your apartment on rue Sainte-Anne wearing an oversize backless sweater like a dress and worn-out Greek sandals. This calls for the right snack—cozy, alluring, not about to weigh you down. Might as well go for it while we're here: crank up the Françoise Hardy and get your pout on.

4 ½-inch-thick slices Pullman loaf or sourdough bread

3 ounces young Fontina cheese, thinly sliced*

3 tablespoons champagne vinegar

½ teaspoon Dijon mustard

¼ cup olive oil

½ teaspoon salt

½ teaspoon freshly ground black pepper

Head of romaine lettuce, coarsely chopped

1 Bosc pear, thinly sliced

¼ cup coarsely chopped mint leaves

2 tablespoons chopped toasted walnuts (see page 9)

1. Preheat the oven to 350°F and line a baking sheet with parchment paper.

2. Arrange the bread slices on the prepared baking sheet, top them with the cheese, and bake about 10 minutes, until the cheese melts and the bread is starting to brown.

3. Meanwhile, make the dressing: Whisk together the vinegar, mustard, oil, salt, and pepper.

4. In a large bowl, toss the romaine, pear, and mint with the dressing.

5. Top the cheesy toasts with the salad, sprinkle them with the walnuts, and serve.

*A little note about young Fontina cheese—it's a softer version of Fontina version that lends to melting very well. Fromi is another great cheese to use for this salad if you prefer something a shade stinkier. The name of the game is Alpine style. Talk to the fromager.

Spinach and Sweet Pea

Though you can make this anytime, the taste here is decidedly summertime. Lemony spinach makes for a bright counterpart to the earthy peas. If you can't find Tallegio, swap it out for Époisses for a kiss of tang. A milder sub would be Brie. And if you want to make the topping into an all-in-one, blend the spinach and pea shoots with the rest of the mixture. Then simply top with pumpkin seeds.

2 cups fresh or frozen peas

8 to 12 fresh mint leaves

1 garlic clove

2 tablespoons olive oil

½ cup cubed Tallegio cheese, rind discarded

Salt to taste

1½ cups baby spinach

1 tablespoon freshly squeezed lemon juice

10 ¼-inch-thick baguette slices, pan-toasted with oil (see page 6)

¼ cup unsalted pumpkin seeds, toasted (see page 9)

1 cup pea shoots

1 or 2 lemons, halved

1. Bring a medium saucepan full of water to a boil. Add the peas and blanch for 1 minute, then drain and run under cold water. (If you're using frozen peas, just run them under hot water for a few seconds to thaw.) Pat dry.

2. In a food processor or using an immersion blender, blend the peas, mint, garlic, and oil. Add the Tallegio and pulse a few more times to incorporate. Leave it a little bit chunky. Season with salt.

3. Toss the spinach with the lemon juice.

4. Spread the pea puree evenly over each toast. Top with a layer of spinach and some pumpkin seeds. Dress with pea shoots. Squeeze lemon liberally over the tops.

WHEN YOU HAVE A VERY SPECIAL TOMATO, MAKE A ... BIG TOMATO TOAST

That tomato that somehow cost you seven, eleven—okay, eleven dollars? Yes. Slice it thick. Slice off an equally thick piece of bread, too, and pan-toast it with olive oil and herbs—basil or thyme or rosemary or oregano (see page 6). Get it nice and golden. Top the herby, crispy, goldy bread with the fatty tomato slice and sprinkle with good salt and a little olive oil.

LUNCH is served.

Carrot Ribbons

Get used to using your vegetable peeler for more than just removing the rough skin from your veggies. It's such a versatile tool, you can use it to make ribbons of all kinds: carrots, zucchini, cucumbers, beets, asparagus, and persimmons. I like doing this because it softens up raw vegetables and allows for fuller coverage of whatever dressing I'm mixing them with. These carrot ribbons get a sweet and tangy application of agave and mustard plus my favorite topper, golden raisins.

1½ teaspoons grainy mustard

2 teaspoons apple cider vinegar

1 teaspoon agave nectar

2 teaspoons freshly squeezed lemon juice

⅓ cup golden raisins

4 teaspoons olive oil

2 large carrots, shaved lengthwise using a peeler

1 cup baby arugula

1 teaspoon lemon zest

6 ¼-inch-thick slices ciabatta, rye, or semolina raisin bread, pan-toasted in oil using the heavy-soaking technique (see page 6)

1. In a medium bowl, whisk together the mustard, vinegar, agave nectar, lemon juice, and raisins. Let sit for 10 minutes. Whisk in the oil.

2. Toss the carrots, arugula, and lemon zest with the marinade and raisins.

3. Top each toast with the carrot salad.

Ricotta Part II: More Flavors

There's a ricotta variety show just waiting for you to join in on. But let's be honest here. Something is stopping you. It's the cheesecloth, isn't it? Remembering to buy it makes the whole ricotta concept annoying. But once you have that, you're good for a lot of ricot.

One ricotta recipe can morph into a million flavors. You can steep herbs in the mixture as it's heating up, whip honey into it after it's strained, or swirl in jam just before serving. Here's the foundation of the Ricotta All-Star team and many, many toasts.

1 quart whole milk

½ cup heavy cream

½ teaspoon salt

2 tablespoons freshly squeezed lemon juice

+ CHEESE CLOTH

1. In a large, heavy saucepan over medium-high heat, bring the milk, cream, and salt to a boil, stirring constantly so it doesn't burn. After the mixture comes to a boil, 10 to 12 minutes, lower the heat to a simmer.

2. Add the lemon juice and keep stirring as the mixture simmers. It should curdle after 2 minutes. The longer you allow the mixture to curdle, the "harder" your cheese will be.

3. Line a sieve or mesh strainer with cheesecloth and place it over a large bowl.

4. Pour the mixture into the lined sieve and set aside to strain for 1 hour. (Same thing here: Strain it longer to make it thicker or for a shorter time to make it thinner. It's a matter of taste.) Discard the liquid and transfer the ricotta to a bowl. Chill until cold.

SALTY RICOTTA

After step 4, mix in 1 or 2 tablespoons grated bottarga and shave some on top.

TARRAGON

In step 1, add 2 fresh tarragon sprigs. Remove them in step 4.

HONEY

In step 4, whip 2 or 3 tablespoons honey.

BLUEBERRY

After step 4, swirl in 3 tablespoons blueberry jam.

Golden Beets and Vadouvan Yogurt

Vadouvan is a Frenchman's take on an Indian curry spice. It is a spice blend that originates from Pondicherry, a town in India with a very strong French presence. You can order it from La Boîte in New York City, a spice shop run by Israeli-born, French-trained chef Lior Lev Sercarz. It has an almost sweet taste to it to accompany earthy notes from the turmeric and mustard powder.

Bunch of baby golden beets (or 2 or 3 larger golden beets)

1 yellow onion, chopped (about 1 cup)

2 tablespoons olive oil, plus more for the bread

1 teaspoon vadouvan spice

1 garlic clove, minced

1 cup plain Greek yogurt

½ teaspoon salt

4 ½-inch-thick slices seeded whole wheat bread

1. Preheat the oven to 400°F.

2. Wrap the baby beets in aluminum foil and roast them for 30 to 35 minutes, or until fork-tender. (If you are using larger beets, roast them for 40 to 45 minutes.) Cool, peel, and slice the beets into ¼- to ½-inch slices.

3. In a large pan over low heat, sauté the onion in the oil for about 20 minutes, until softened. When it begins to caramelize, add ½ teaspoon of the vadouvan and continue caramelizing for 15 minutes. Add the garlic and sauté 5 to 7 more minutes, or until the garlic is softened considerably and the onion is well caramelized. Let cool.

4. In a small bowl, combine the yogurt, salt, and cooled onion.

5. In the same pan over high heat, add more oil and pan-toast the bread, 2 minutes per side, sprinkling each side with the remaining ½ teaspoon vadouvan.

6. Spread the oniony yogurt on the toasts and top with the beet rounds.

Fennel Parmesan Slaw

This recipe needs a mandoline. You really should get one. The one I have cost forty dollars and it's lasted me eight years . . . *so far.* If you did not learn paper-thin slicing skills in culinary school—as I didn't—go for the mandoline. Simply run the vegetable of your choice back and forth against the blade and out come translucent wisps. For this recipe it's essential, unless you have a lot of time for hand slicing and you're a certified slicing savant. But if you ask me, there are better ways to work up an appetite. ♥

1 small fennel bulb

1 medium apple, preferably Pink Lady or Honeycrisp, cored

2 ounces Parmesan

2 tablespoons pomegranate seeds

3 tablespoons freshly squeezed lime juice

2 tablespoons freshly squeezed lemon juice

6 ¼-inch-thick slices rustic Italian or ciabatta, pan-toasted with mayo (see page 7)

1. Using your mandoline, slice the fennel, apple, and Parmesan into ⅛-inch-thick slices. They should be almost translucent. The Parmesan might crumble, and that's okay. Place in a medium bowl.

2. Add the pomegranate seeds, lime juice, and lemon juice to the bowl with the fennel, apple, and Parmesan. Toss lightly.

3. Mound ½ cup of slaw onto each toast and serve.

I don't add any oil or fat to the slaw because I like the fresh flavor of citrus and citrus only. Adding 1 tablespoon olive oil won't hurt, though, and you might prefer this for a rounder flavor.

Shaved Asparagus and Serrano-Basil Butter

MAKES 8 TOASTS, WITH EXTRA SERRANO-BASIL BUTTER

There's not a great way to make a little bit of spicy butter, so make a stick and keep it on hand in the fridge for spreading on corn bread and to perk up some mellow roasted vegetables. Any way you use it, it sets the tone for a mouthwatering night.

8 tablespoons (1 stick) salted butter, softened

2 serrano peppers, chopped, with seeds for spicy-spicy, without for normal spicy

10 basil leaves

2 tablespoons lime zest

Bunch of asparagus (jumbo, if possible), trimmed

¼ cup chopped cilantro

2 tablespoons freshly squeezed lime juice

1 tablespoon olive oil

⅛ teaspoon salt

8 ¼-inch-thick slices crusty tangy white bread or miche, oven-toasted until golden (see page 8)

1. With an immersion blender, mix the butter, peppers, basil, and lime zest until the peppers are broken up. Set aside.

2. Using a vegetable peeler, shave the asparagus lengthwise into long strands. Toss in a large bowl with the cilantro, lime juice, oil, and salt.

3. Spread the butter evenly on each toast (about 2 teaspoons per slice). Top with the asparagus salad and serve.

White Bean Avo

Another avocado toast variant? Yes, indeed. When you smash it with white beans and herbs, a whole new flavor emerges. Praise.

5 tablespoons olive oil

2 garlic cloves, thinly sliced

3 or 4 fresh basil leaves

1 teaspoon chopped oregano

1 teaspoon chopped thyme

1 15-ounce can cannellini beans, rinsed and drained

1 ripe avocado, pitted and peeled

1 teaspoon freshly squeezed lemon juice

½ teaspoon onion powder

1 teaspoon salt

½ teaspoon freshly ground black pepper

6 ½-inch-thick slices 7-grain bread

Pinch of cayenne, chili powder, or shichimi togarashi

1. In a small pan over medium heat, heat the oil and garlic and sauté until the garlic is crispy, about 3 minutes.

2. Transfer the garlic to a paper towel to dry. Let the oil cool in the pan.

3. When the oil is cooled slightly, use an immersion blender to blend it with the basil, oregano, and thyme. (If you want to do it by hand, chop the herbs very finely and combine them with the oil in a bowl.)

4. In a medium bowl, mash together the beans, avocado, lemon juice, onion powder, salt, pepper, and 1 tablespoon of the herb oil. Set aside.

5. Pan-toast the bread in the remaining herb-garlic oil until golden, 2 minutes per side (see page 6).

6. Spread the avocado-bean mixture evenly on the toasts. Top with the garlic chips and a light sprinkle of cayenne.

Mushroom Hunks

Some girls remember outfits; I remember meals. I had a very hunky mushroom toast in Chelsea several years ago and then daydreamed about it until I had reason to make it myself. It's simple yet luscious—a stud of a toast.

8 tablespoons (1 stick) unsalted butter

Leaves from 4 thyme sprigs (about 2 teaspoons)

6 1-inch slices miche or rustic Italian bread

12 ounces hen-of-the-woods, chanterelle, and oyster mushrooms, cut into large pieces

½ teaspoon salt

1. In a small bowl, blend the butter and thyme with a fork until well incorporated.

2. Spread half of the thyme butter on both sides of the bread slices. In a medium pan over medium heat, pan-toast the bread (see page 7). Set the toasts aside.

3. To the same pan over medium heat, add the remaining butter mixture and sauté the mushrooms in batches until well browned, 3 to 4 minutes per batch, taking care not to crowd the pan.

4. In a medium bowl, mix together the mushroom batches and season with the salt.

5. Pile onto the toasts and devour.

ROOTS

The general concept is this: You slow-roast some root vegetables—of a kind or a variety. Butternut squash, Delicata, kabocha, and turnips all work really well. Carrots and parsnips, too. Roast them with olive oil and garlic and a few herbs. When they are good and mushy, blend them with oil until you've got a thick puree. Spread that on your toast. Then add some simple toppings.

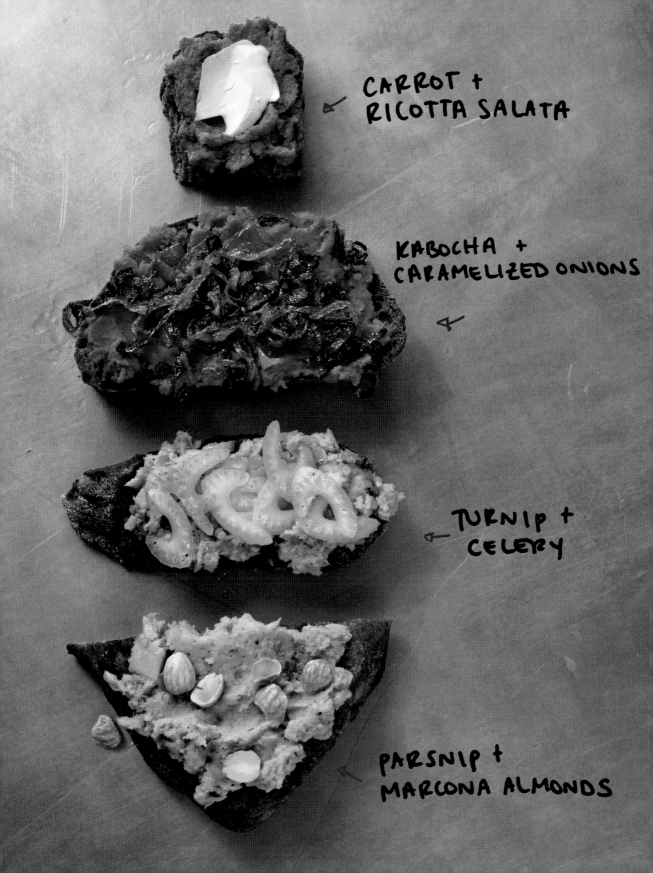

CARROT +
RICOTTA SALATA

KABOCHA +
CARAMELIZED ONIONS

TURNIP +
CELERY

PARSNIP +
MARCONA ALMONDS

Cucumber Tzatziki and Roasted Jalapeños

Roasting peppers brings a sweetness to their spice. The tzatziki acts as a cooling agent and works great as a dip for vegetables. Chop up the jalapeños, add them to the dip, and use as a base for chicken or shrimp salad or to eat with pita chips.

4 ounces silken tofu

1 tablespoon freshly squeezed lemon juice

½ garlic clove

½ teaspoon onion powder

¼ teaspoon freshly ground black pepper

½ cup plain Greek yogurt

1 cup julienned cucumber (peeled, halved crosswise, and seeded first)

¼ cup minced dill

6 jalapeños

½ teaspoon salt

8 ½-inch-thick slices pumpernickel bread, oven-toasted with oil (see page 8)

1. Preheat the oven to broil, set an oven rack on the highest level, and line a baking sheet with parchment paper.

2. Make the tzatziki: Using an immersion blender or a food processor, puree the tofu, lemon juice, garlic, onion powder, and pepper. Fold in the yogurt, cucumber, and dill.

3. Stem the jalapeños, cut them into quarters lengthwise, and remove the seeds. Place them skin side up on the prepared baking sheet, sprinkle with salt, and roast them on the top rack of the oven for 7 to 10 minutes, until blistery.

4. Top each toast with a heap of the tzatziki and 3 of the blistered jalapeño slices.

Delicata Squash and Orange Butter

This is a party toast. Pan-toasting the bread in orange butter makes for an extraspecial delivery system for wine-soaked raisins. Serve these toasts at the table prebuilt or as a build-your-own.

2 Delicata squash

4 tablespoons olive oil

¼ teaspoon salt

1 tablespoon honey

⅓ cup golden raisins

¼ cup white wine

1 shallot, minced (about 3 tablespoons)

1 cup freshly squeezed orange juice

5 tablespoons unsalted butter

2 tablespoons freshly squeezed lemon juice

8 ½-inch-thick slices rye bread

1. Preheat the oven to 350°F and line a baking sheet with parchment paper.

2. Cut the squash in half lengthwise. Remove the seeds and slice the squash into ½-inch-thick half-moons (keep the rind on).

3. Spread the squash on the prepared baking sheet and sprinkle the pieces with 2 tablespoons of the oil and the salt and drizzle them with the honey. Roast the squash until soft, about 25 minutes.

4. Meanwhile, in a small bowl, soak the raisins in the wine. Set aside.

5. In a small saucepan over medium heat, sauté the shallot in the remaining 2 tablespoons oil until softened, about 4 minutes. Add the wine and raisins and cook until the wine has evaporated, 2 to 4 minutes. Toss the shallots and raisins with the squash in a medium bowl.

6. In the same small saucepan over medium heat, hard simmer the orange juice until it has reduced to ¼ cup, 7 to 10 minutes. Stir in the butter and lemon juice. Let cool.

7. Spread half the orange butter on both sides of the bread and pan-toast in a medium skillet for 2 minutes. Flip and pan-toast for another 2 minutes, until golden brown.

8. Arrange the squash on the toasts. Serve with the rest of the orange butter.

Carrot Butter and Halloumi

MAKES 4 TOASTS, WITH EXTRA BUTTER

Smoked paprika makes this toast nuanced and earthy. Omit it if you want a cleaner, brighter flavor and add a squeeze of lemon. Use the extra butter for carrot cake (sans paprika), corn bread, sweet potatoes, baked potatoes, or roasted cippolini. Use it as a rub for pork or chicken, or melt it over Brussels sprouts or blanched green beans. And halloumi . . . you know, it's the cheese you can grill. If you can stash away any extra, grill it and top with fig jam for breakfast.

2 or 3 large carrots, peeled and roughly chopped (about 2 cups)

2 shallots, roughly chopped

5 tablespoons olive oil

5 tablespoons unsalted butter

2 tablespoons goat cheese

¼ teaspoon smoked paprika, plus more for garnish (optional)

½ teaspoon salt

1 teaspoon freshly ground black pepper

Squeeze of lemon (optional)

4 ounces halloumi cheese

4 ¾-inch-thick slices whole grain, seedy bread or dark rye, toasted using the plain-old-toast technique (see page 8)

1. Preheat the oven to 350°F and line a baking sheet with parchment paper.

2. On the prepared baking sheet, toss the carrots and shallots in 3 tablespoons of the oil. Bake for 30 to 35 minutes, until soft. Let cool.

3. In a food processor, blend the carrots, shallots, butter, goat cheese, paprika (if using), salt, and pepper until smooth. A squeeze of lemon is nice here if you have it on hand.

4. Slice the halloumi into four ½-inch-thick slabs. Brush both sides of the slabs with the remaining 2 tablespoons oil. In a small pan or grill pan over medium-high heat, sear the halloumi, 1 or 2 minutes per side, or until it develops a golden-brown shell.

5. Spread about 1 tablespoon of the carrot butter on each toast and top with one halloumi slice. Sprinkle with a little more paprika (if using) for prettiness.

Chipotle Eggplant

If today is not the day to go outside, if it's gray and kind of damp-cold . . . if it's a movie day or maybe a day to reread *Dune* or some Roald Dahl . . . if it's *whatever,* then it's definitely a day to use the can of chipotles in adobo that has been in the pantry since two Thanksgivings ago, when they were mashed with sweet potatoes.

WHY did I think I'd use two full cans?! (I used like half of one.)

Use it with eggplant now on a toast that's good hot or cold, in a recipe that has a lot of downtime for reading or movie watching or tie-dyeing your curtains.

3 tablespoons olive oil

1 large white onion, chopped (about 2 cups)

1 medium eggplant, cubed (3½ to 4 cups)

¼ cup white wine (optional)

2 tablespoons chopped canned chipotle chiles in adobo (1 or 2 peppers) with their sauce

¼ teaspoon ground cinnamon

¼ teaspoon salt

6 2-inch-thick slices white bread or Pullman loaf, pan-toasted with mayo (see page 7)

Maldon smoked sea salt

1. In a medium pan over medium-low heat, heat the oil. Add the onion and eggplant and sauté until soft, about 35 minutes. If using wine, add it and let it cook off, 10 more minutes (otherwise, just let cook about 45 minutes total). Stir occasionally while cooking.

2. Add the chipotle peppers and their bit of sauce, the cinnamon, and the salt. Turn the heat to low and sauté another 20 minutes, or until the peppers are broken down and the mixture is thickened.

3. To serve, top the toasts with the eggplant mixture and a sprinkle of Maldon smoked salt.

Cauliflower Melts

Raisins have a long shelf life and are great for a boost of energy. I was walking on a cold boardwalk, quite a ways from home, when a pang of hunger attacked. I was wearing my ski jacket—an ideal jacket for the beach in the winter and also ideal for storage with its plentiful pockets for goggles, headphones, keys, money, credit cards, lip balm, sunblock, and Starburst. There are always a few raisins tucked away somewhere (long pocket life?), too; same in this recipe—hidden and sweetly surprising.

¼ cup olive oil

2 garlic cloves, minced

1 teaspoon salt

½ teaspoon freshly ground pepper

Medium head of cauliflower, cut into ½-inch-thick slabs, possibly halved to make a total of 8 slabs

½ cup golden raisins

¼ cup white wine (optional)

¼ cup shelled pistachios

8 ½-inch-thick slices sourdough bread

4 ounces Comté or Manchego cheese, cut into 8 slices

2 tablespoons chopped parsley

1. Preheat the oven to 350°F and line a baking sheet with parchment paper.

2. In a medium bowl, combine the oil, garlic, salt, and pepper. Add the cauliflower slabs and toss to coat.

3. Arrange the cauliflower on the prepared baking sheet. Bake for 25 minutes, flip the slabs, and bake another 10 to 20 minutes, until softened and roasty. Set aside to cool but keep the oven on.

4. Meanwhile, in a small bowl, soak the raisins in wine or water for 10 minutes. Drain.

5. In a small pan over medium-high heat, toast the pistachios, dry or with a little oil. Let cool on a paper towel, then chop coarsely.

6. Lay the bread on the baking sheet and arrange the cauliflower on the bread, cutting it to fit as needed. Sprinkle with the pistachios and raisins and top with the cheese.

7. Bake until the cheese melts, 7 to 10 minutes.

8. Top the toasts with the parsley and serve immediately.

Walnut Potatoasts

Today, do the crossword and make potatoes. The *New York Times* crossword. Yukon Gold potatoes. They're hard at first, but then they warm up. And the more you eat potatoes on toast, the more you'll want them. Ditto the puzzle: addictive. Even if you can't complete it, you get an A for effort, but don't worry, these potatoes are as easy as a Monday puzzle.

¼ cup walnuts

5 tablespoons olive oil

10 baby Yukon Gold potatoes, sliced

¾ teaspoon salt

1 teaspoon freshly ground black pepper

6 ¾-inch-thick slices pumpernickel bread

⅔ cup crème fraîche

Parsley, for garnish

1. In a medium pan over medium heat, toast the walnuts in the oil until browned, 2 to 4 minutes. Remove the nuts with a slotted spoon to drain and cool on a paper towel. Reserve the oil in the pan. Chop the nuts when cool.

2. Preheat the oven to 375°F and line a baking sheet with parchment paper.

3. Toss the potatoes in 2 tablespoons of the reserved walnut oil, ½ teaspoon of the salt, and ¾ teaspoon of the pepper. Spread the potatoes on the baking sheet and roast until golden, 25 to 30 minutes.

4. Pan-toast the bread in the remaining 3 tablespoons reserved walnut oil until crisp, about 2 minutes per side, adding more oil if necessary so as not to burn the bread.

5. Mix the walnuts into the crème fraîche. Season with the remaining ¼ teaspoon salt and ¼ teaspoon pepper.

6. Top each toast with 6 to 8 potato slices and 1½ tablespoons crème fraîche. Garnish with parsley and serve.

Feel like waiting 'til later to eat? This toast at room temp might give a second wave of inspiration . . . like adding capers, or bottarga: you just Microplane it over this toast to up the ante (which is totally a *Times* word).

Brown Sugar Chipotle Sweet Potato and Carrot

Another great use for the extra chipotles in adobo in your cupboard (see page 150)—smashing them with goat cheese makes them highly cravable. Revisit the spread later with black beans and red quinoa wrapped up in blanched kale with a little cilantro. Or try it smeared on a warm corn tortilla.

2 or 3 large carrots, sliced into ½-inch-thick coins (about 2 cups)

1 large sweet potato, peeled, cut into ½-inch-thick rounds, then quartered (about 2 cups)

3 tablespoons brown sugar

2 garlic cloves, minced

1 teaspoon ground cumin

¼ teaspoon salt

3 tablespoons olive oil

6 ounces goat cheese, softened

2 tablespoons canned chopped chipotle chiles in adobo with their sauce

8 ½-inch-thick slices raisin bread

1. Preheat the oven to 350°F and line a baking sheet with parchment paper.

2. In a large bowl, toss the carrots and sweet potato with the sugar, garlic, cumin, salt, and oil.

3. Spread the veggies evenly on the prepared baking sheet and roast for 40 to 45 minutes, until soft. Move them around a bit with a spatula after 20 minutes so they do not burn.

4. Meanwhile, in a small bowl, mix the goat cheese and chipotle peppers with a fork until well blended.

5. Spread about 3 tablespoons of the cheese on each piece of bread and lay them on a baking sheet. Toast the bread in the oven for the last 10 minutes with the veggies.

6. Top the toasts with the carrots and sweets and serve.

Butternut Squash, Robiola, and Apples

You're buying a whole butternut squash for this recipe, so you're going to have some choices to make. After you've roasted it, you can reserve some chunks for eating whole, tossing with black rice, or dipping in ketchup (think butternut oven fries). Or you could puree the squash entirely and reserve some for serving with warm scallops simply seared and placed on top. You can thin out the puree with some cream or milk and stir it into gemelli pasta with spinach and sautéed garlic. Or make a ton of these toasts and make a lot of people happy all at once. Serve up some Humboldt Fog and chunks of Parmesan on the side.

1 butternut squash (about 3 pounds)

Olive oil

16 sage leaves

4 garlic cloves

½ teaspoon salt

½ teaspoon freshly ground black pepper

6 ¾-inch-thick slices sourdough bread

1 Pink Lady apple, cored and thinly sliced

4 ounces Robiola or any soft, creamy cheese. *

1. Preheat the oven to 400°F and line a baking sheet with parchment paper.

2. Peel the butternut squash, seed it, and cut it into roughly 2-inch cubes.

3. In a medium bowl, toss the squash with 4 tablespoons of the oil, 3 or 4 chopped sage leaves, the garlic, salt, and pepper.

4. Spread the squash mixture on the baking sheet and roast for 20 to 30 minutes, until soft. Let it cool on the baking sheet.

5. Meanwhile, make the fried sage by heating 1 inch of the oil in a medium pan over medium heat. Drop in the remaining sage leaves and fry until crisp, about 60 seconds. Set aside on a paper towel.

*Robiola is mild and a little tangy.

6. In the sage oil, pan-toast the bread over high heat until golden brown, about 2 minutes per side (see page 6).

7. Puree the squash mixture in a blender until smooth, adding up to 4 tablespoons sage oil (or regular olive oil if your sage oil is used up), 1 tablespoon at a time, to achieve a smooth, thick puree.

8. Spread about 2 tablespoons of puree on each toast and top with 3 or 4 apple slices. Dollop with the Robiola and garnish with the fried sage.

Roasted Eggplant and Raisin Chutney

Kind of a quasi-deconstructed classic caponata, there's no better thing to put on toast. Eggplant has been snuggling up with warm bread since Romeo loved Juliet. There's something to be said for opposites attracting. Sweet, salty, smooth, sour . . . love at first bite. A caponata by any other name tastes just as sweet.

¼ cup raisins

¼ cup white wine

1 medium eggplant

5 tablespoons olive oil

¼ teaspoon salt

⅛ teaspoon freshly ground black pepper

1 large shallot, minced (about ½ cup)

1 tablespoon tomato paste

1 tablespoon red wine vinegar

2 teaspoons lemon zest

¼ cup toasted pine nuts (see page 9)

10 ¼-inch-thick slices wheat baguette, cut on a severe bias with pointy edges, and oven-toasted with oil (see page 8)

1. Preheat the oven to 350°F and line a baking sheet with parchment paper.

2. In a small bowl, soak the raisins in the wine.

3. Slice the eggplant into ten ½-inch rounds and then slice them in half. In a large bowl, toss with 3 tablespoons of the oil, the salt, and the pepper.

4. Lay the rounds on the prepared baking sheet and roast for 25 to 30 minutes, until soft.

5. Meanwhile, make the chutney: In a small pan over medium heat, sauté the shallot in the remaining 2 tablespoons oil for 15 minutes, until very soft. Add the tomato paste. Give it a stir and then add the raisins with wine and the vinegar. Let the wine cook off, 2 to 4 minutes. Remove from the heat and add the lemon zest.

6. Mix the pine nuts into the chutney.

7. Top each piece of toast with 2 eggplant half-moons and 1 tablespoon chutney.

SERVE WITH A SIDE OF LEMONY ARUGULA!

Hot Brussels Sprouts

Keep this mixture on hand and make a dinner toast at the end of the day, scooping a hefty portion onto sturdy bread and heating the whole thing up in the oven or toaster oven. These and a glass of white . . . when you and your BFF decide to finally sit down and watch *The Wire*. Aw shiiiiiiit.

2 tablespoons olive oil

3 shallots, chopped (about 1 cup)

3 garlic cloves, chopped

3 cups trimmed, roughly chopped Brussels sprouts

3 tablespoons cream cheese

⅓ cup mayonnaise

1 large egg white

1 cup grated Parmesan

3 sage leaves, chopped

½ teaspoon cayenne

½ teaspoon salt

½ teaspoon freshly ground black pepper

6 ½-inch-thick slices white Pullman loaf or Quinoa-Millet Bread (see page 11)

1. Preheat the oven to 350°F and line a baking sheet with parchment paper.

2. In a medium skillet over medium heat, heat the oil and sauté the shallots and garlic until soft, about 5 minutes. Add the Brussels sprouts and sauté 4 to 5 more minutes, or until soft. Let cool.

3. In a bowl, combine the Brussels sprouts mixture, cream cheese, mayonnaise, egg white, ⅓ cup of the Parmesan, the sage, cayenne, salt, and pepper.

4. Spread the mixture on each piece of bread, sprinkle with the remaining ⅔ cup Parmesan to cover, and arrange on the prepared baking sheet.

5. Bake for 15 to 20 minutes, or until the cheese forms a golden shell on top. Serve hot.

Spicy Red Lentil

Spending time in India led to a love of lentils, not to mention turmeric and cumin. Everything in India is highly spiced, not to say it's spicy. This toast has added personality from the sriracha, but you can choose your preferred level of heat. The spread should be spoonable.

½ cup red lentils

1 yellow onion, diced (about 1 cup)

1 teaspoon ground cumin

2 teaspoons ground turmeric

½ teaspoon garlic powder

2 tablespoons olive oil

3 tablespoons coarse cornmeal

⅓ cup tomato sauce

1 to 2 tablespoons sriracha (heat to your taste)

1 teaspoon red chili pepper flakes

½ teaspoon salt

½ teaspoon freshly ground black pepper

4 teaspoons freshly squeezed lemon juice

1 teaspoon lemon zest

¼ cup plain Greek yogurt

6 ¼-inch-thick slices walnut wheat bread, pan-toasted with oil (see page 6)

2 tablespoons chopped cilantro and/or mint

1. In a small saucepan over medium heat, cook the lentils in 1 cup water, covered, until the water is absorbed and the lentils are soft, about 20 minutes.

2. In a medium saucepan over medium heat, sauté the onion, cumin, turmeric, and garlic powder in the oil until softened, about 5 minutes. Add the lentils and cornmeal and cook, stirring, until thickened, about 2 minutes. Add the tomato sauce, sriracha, and chili flakes and cook for 3 to 4 minutes, or until thickened. Mix in the salt, pepper, and 2 teaspoons of the lemon juice.

3. In a small bowl, combine the remaining 2 teaspoons lemon juice, the lemon zest, and the yogurt.

4. Top the bread with red lentil mash, a dollop of citrus yogurt, and the chopped herbs.

Spiced Apple Chutney

When you make this chutney, the rate at which the apples cook and the cooking liquid evaporates will depend not only on the heat of the stove but also on the season, the weather, and the humidity. Watch it! Add water as you go if the apples need more time to soften. Once you've mastered that, you can do this toast any which way.

2 apples, such as Pink Lady, Honeycrisp, or Fuji, cored and cut into ¾-inch dice

2 tablespoons turbinado sugar

¼ cup white wine

¼ cup raisins

1 cinnamon stick

2 cloves

½ teaspoon freshly ground black pepper

1 ½-inch-long fresh ginger knob, peeled

1 1-inch-long piece orange rind

2 teaspoons freshly squeezed lemon juice

4 ½-inch-thick slices semolina-raisin bread

4 ounces Moses Sleeper* or Havarti, Gouda, or Muenster cheese

1. Preheat the oven to 350°F.

2. In a medium pot over medium-high heat, combine the apples, sugar, wine, raisins, cinnamon stick, cloves, pepper, ginger, orange rind, and lemon juice. Bring to a boil, then reduce the heat so the chutney stays at a simmer; cook until the apples are tender, 30 to 40 minutes. Add ¼ cup water after 20 minutes if the liquid has evaporated completely and the apples aren't yet cooked.

3. On a baking sheet, oven-toast the bread, dry (i.e., make plain old toast; see page 8), until golden, about 10 minutes.

4. As soon as the toasts come out of the oven, put a ½-inch slice of cheese on each toast so it gets a touch melty.

5. Top each toast with 2 tablespoons of apple chutney and serve.

*Moses Sleeper is a cheese made at Jasper Hill Farm in Vermont. It's buttery and a little cruciferous-tasting; fresh and earthy like Camembert.

6 extra bread

Panzanella

Maple-Pear Bread Pudding

Honey-Citrus Sundae Toast

Lemon-Lavender Sweet Toast

Midnight Snacks

Watermelon

INGREDIENTS STILL LINGER BUT THE BREAD IS STALE : IT'S PANZANELLA TIME

The debris from making several toasts lends itself quite well to toast in another form: salad. While bread acts as the base in a toast, it's fully incorporated in panzanella. Some people follow the tear-and-toast technique; others cube and bake. Either way, make sure your bread pieces are bite-size. Use the recipes in this book as a guide to inspire flavor combinations.

1. Preheat the oven to 350°F and line a baking sheet with parchment paper.

2. Cut or rip your bread of choice—go ahead and use the remainder of the stale bread you have lying around—into 1- or 2-inch pieces.

3. Toss the bread with olive oil, salt, and pepper. Toss it with other dried herbs and spices like sumac, paprika, onion powder, togarashi, or cayenne if you'd like. Place it evenly on the baking sheet and bake for 10 to 12 minutes, or until crisped.

4. Meanwhile, throw the other panzanella components (see below for several suggestions) in a large bowl and toss with whatever "dressing" ingredients are included in the recipe (or that you have on hand).

5. Add the bread, mix to incorporate, and serve.

A FEW EXAMPLES:

• Rosemary roasted grapes . . . add some arugula and bread bites, toss with honey and balsamic, and dot with a blend of goat and blue cheeses (from page 72)

• Seared tuna, tatsoi, watermelon radishes, extra crispy bread . . . sprinkle with black sesame seeds, scallions, rice wine vinegar, olive oil, and a little sesame oil and soy sauce (from page 76)

• Zucchini, celery, slices of bottarga, grated Parmesan, and cubed bread . . . toss with lemon and olive oil (from page 111)

• Spice roasted radishes, radish greens, toasted pine nuts, mint, and torn bread . . . toss with mint feta yogurt (from page 120)

• Brown sugar carrots and sweet potatoes . . . add chopped romaine and soft baked cubed bread, toss with olive oil and a little lemon, and dollop with the spicy cheese (from page 156)

Maple-Pear Bread Pudding

MAKES 8 TO 12 SERVINGS

When you have leftover soft bread, like brioche, challah, or pain de mie, bread pudding is in order. It's toast's sloppy cousin.

This bread pudding needs to firm up for at least an hour and up to 24 hours before baking, so it's a great make-ahead brunch dish. Or start it and then go get a drink while you wait.

8 1-inch-thick slices challah bread

2 very ripe Bartlett pears, cored, peeled, and sliced ½ inch thick (reserve cores and skin)

⅔ cup plus 5 tablespoons turbinado sugar

3 cups whole milk

3 tablespoons maple syrup

4 large eggs

½ teaspoon ground cinnamon, plus more for dusting

¼ teaspoon ground ginger

½ teaspoon pure vanilla extract

¼ teaspoon salt

2 tablespoons unsalted butter, plus more for the pan

¾ cup hazelnuts, roasted and skinned*

1 star anise (optional)

1. Butter a 10-inch loaf pan. Vertically layer the challah slices with the pear slices in between, as if you're reconstructing the loaf, until the pan is full.

2. In a medium saucepan, add the reserved pear cores and skins, 3 tablespoons of the sugar, and enough water to cover the mixture (about 1 cup). Cover and simmer for 25 minutes over low heat. Strain the mixture into a bowl and reserve the syrup until needed.

3. In a medium saucepan over medium heat, bring the milk, the ⅔ cup sugar, and the maple syrup almost to a boil, then turn the heat to low and stir until the sugar is dissolved, 2 to 3 minutes. Let cool slightly.

(continued)

To roast and skin the nuts, roast them on a rimmed baking sheet at 350°F for about 10 minutes, or until browned. Gather them into a dishcloth. Wrap up the towel and rub or roll it against the counter to remove the skins.

FOR THOSE
SOFT BREAD
SCRAPS →

4. Meanwhile, beat the eggs with the cinnamon, ginger, vanilla, and salt. Slowly add the egg mixture to the milk mixture, stirring constantly and taking care not to cook the eggs. Stop as needed to let the mixtures become friends. *Don't get them angry.*

5. Pour the mixture over the bread and pears to cover. Don't overfill (let the liquid absorb into the bread); discard any extra mixture. Cover and let it set up in the fridge for at least 1 hour but up to 24 hours. The longer it sits, the better.

6. When ready to bake, preheat the oven to 375°F.

7. In a small saucepan over medium heat, heat the butter, the remaining 2 tablespoons sugar, and the hazelnuts. Sauté until the hazelnuts are browned and the sugar-butter is sticking to the nuts, 3 or 4 minutes. Spread the nuts out on parchment paper and set aside to cool. Chop when cooled. (You can do this step at any point while the bread pudding is setting up and hold the hazelnuts at room temp.)

8. Put the star anise (if using) in the middle of the bread pudding. Bake for 55 to 65 minutes, until the bread is puffy and the liquid is absorbed. If the top isn't crispy, crank up the oven heat for 5 minutes to get it there.

9. Let the bread pudding cool for about 5 minutes before serving. Scoop or slice it onto plates, drizzle with warm pear syrup, and top with the candied hazelnuts and a dusting of cinnamon.

FOR USING UP HARDER BREAD:

Honey-Citrus Sundae Toast

MAKES 4 SUNDAES

In summer 2007, I found myself at a friend of a friend of a friend's three-day, never-get-dark birthday celebration at an opulent, floating banquet hall on the pristine blue water surrounding St. Petersburg, Russia. During those twenty-four-hour days, I got to know Sasha, and a few days later at her sister's Moscow apartment, after a vigorous branch beating at her local *banya* (pictures to prove it), Sasha grabbed a brick of vanilla ice cream from the freezer and sliced off three butterlike sticks for us. I asked why the ice cream came in thinly wrapped blocks and not the usual carton. She mumbled something about USSR-era blandness and added that during that time vanilla or, rather, "plain" was the only option. She then proceeded to dress up the 'scream with ribbons of honey, fresh lemon juice, and finally zest that mimicked sprinkles. My delight over this treat delighted them, and when they told me that this was what they grew up with, I was overcome with admiration and respect for their savvy. Nothing could keep two sweets-loving sisters from a Soviet-squashing sundae. Eat this combination on a slice of buttered bread, another simple luxury that somehow goes very, very well.

1 pint vanilla ice cream

4 slices ciabatta or baguette, pan-
toasted with butter (see page 7)

4 tablespoons honey

2 teaspoons freshly squeezed lemon juice

2 teaspoons lemon zest

1. Scoop the ice cream onto the bread slices.

2. Drizzle with the honey and lemon juice. Sprinkle with the lemon zest.

Lemon-Lavender Sweet Toast

If toast toast wasn't enough and you want dessert bread, toasted.

10 tablespoons (1 stick plus 2 tablespoons) unsalted butter, at room temperature

4 tablespoons olive oil

1 cup plus 2 tablespoons turbinado sugar

¼ cup packed light brown sugar

⅓ cup whole milk

2½ teaspoons lavender

3 large eggs

1½ teaspoons pure vanilla extract

1¾ cups all-purpose flour

½ teaspoon baking powder

½ teaspoon salt

¼ teaspoon ground ginger

2 tablespoons lemon zest

¼ cup plus 1 teaspoon freshly squeezed lemon juice

⅓ cup mascarpone

1. Preheat the oven to 350°F and oil or butter a 10-inch loaf pan.

2. In a standing mixer, blend the butter, oil, 1 cup turbinado sugar, and the brown sugar for *a full* 7 minutes, until light and creamy.

3. Meanwhile, in a small saucepan over very low heat, simmer the milk with the lavender for 5 to 10 minutes, taking care not to scald the milk. Nestle a piece of cheesecloth in a strainer over a bowl. Strain the milk into the bowl and set the milk in the fridge to cool. Discard the lavender.

4. Add the eggs and vanilla to the sugar-butter mixture and mix until just incorporated.

5. In another bowl, mix the flour, baking powder, salt, ginger, zest, and ¼ cup lemon juice.

6. Mix half the flour mixture into the wet ingredients to incorporate. Then mix in the remainder of the flour mixture and the lavender milk.

7. Pour the batter into the prepared loaf pan and sprinkle the top with the remaining 2 tablespoons turbinado sugar.

8. Bake for 1 hour, then check for doneness (the cake should be bouncy). Bake another 10 minutes or so if necessary. Let cool, then slice.

9. In a small bowl, mix the mascarpone with the 1 teaspoon lemon juice.

10. To serve, toast the slices, plain old toast style (see page 8), and spread with mascarpone.

ROCK-HARD LEFTOVER SLICES?
PAN-TOAST UNTIL FULLY CRISPED
AND SERVE WITH CREAMY, OOZY, GOOEY
BURRATA.

SALTY SNACKS AND SWEET DREAMS

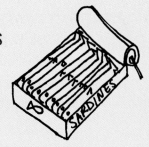

Dry-toast bread in a toaster, slather on a thick layer of butter, and . . .
- grate on enough bottarga to cover the butter.
- mash in canned sardines with their oil.
- top with 2 or 3 anchovies.

PRE-BREAKFAST IN BED

Spread preserves on bread, cover the preserves with cheese, and toast in a toaster oven until the cheese bubbles.
- Blackberry preserves + mozzarella
- Orange marmalade + pecorino
- Strawberry preserves + fresh goat cheese
- Peach preserves + cottage cheese (with this one, add the cottage cheese after toasting)

A HEAD START ON CHEESE TOAST: SNEAKING ANOTHER SLICE

Plain slice + sautéed eggplant + sautéed shallots + spinach
Pepperoni slice + sautéed Brussels sprouts + pecorino
Mushroom slice + sunny-side-up egg + sriracha

Midnight Snacks

Technically, it's always toast time. But midnight gets a special prize as the perfect hour for a sliced bread break. Be grateful you've got some left on hand.

Salty sea snacks with a little butter make for an ideal savory presleep sedative. Fruit preserves and meltable cheese are dreamy. And if all you have is pizza from earlier in the evening, you can count that as toast, too. It's dark out; no one will know.

IF YOU THOUGHT THAT
THIS BOOK WAS
ABOUT BUBBLY TOASTS,
HERE'S ALL YOU NEED
TO KNOW: SPEND
YOUR EXTRA BREAD ON
BILLECART-SALMON AND
DRINK WITH WATERMELON.
AND GOOD BUDDIES. (—D)

acknowledgments

Mom, Dad, Jeffrey, and Jason, I love you, and thanks for everything—unconditional love, believing in me, unabashed feedback, and being such a wonderful family.

I wouldn't have been able to write the book without help. Thank you, Cassie Jones, editor extraordinaire. Thank you so much, Kari Stuart and Tommy Cohen.

An awesome photography team deserves awesome thanks: John Von Pamer (photographer), Erin McDowell (food stylist), and Brian Heiser (prop stylist), and our wonderful support team, Khadija Khansia, Ladan Liban, Remy Albert, Anna Spangler, Rachel Cleary, Emma Hede-Brierley, Julie Tanous, and Cora Thomas. Thank you, Michelli Knauer, for jumping in to style the cover.

Thank you for your generosity, support, and dot connecting: Richard Teichman, Larry Mufson, Betsy Fillmore, and Louise Eastman. Kerrilynn Pamer, Joy Wilson, Dany Levy, Griffin Dunne, Sebastian Hue, Taylor Thompson, Jesse Salazar, Moira Sedgwick, and Sandy Stillman.

Thanks to recipe testers Carly Gould, Katie Han, Sarah Chang, Jen Heringhausen, Elizabeth Barnes, Julie Deciantis, Jane Frye, Laurel Lyman, Megan Gottig, Derek Laughren, and all of the Culinistas.

Cred to Shabd Simon-Alexander: thank you for your beautiful dyed silks.

Cred to the bakeries Runner & Stone, Amy's Bread, Bien Cuit, Bruce Young from Salisbury Breads, Orwashers, Maison Kayser, and Breads Bakery as well as Good Eggs. Service Smoked Fish, Guido's Fresh Marketplace, and the Lobster Place for excellent quality seafood and service: thank you.

A Polaroid is the photo equivalent of a toast—it's quick, portable, and single serving. Shooting with a Polaroid camera is ephemeral and chancy. It's whimsical and simple. Like a piece of toast, a Polaroid picture is nostalgic and makes anyone smile. The Polaroid shots were taken using a classic, low-tech Polaroid camera until mine broke; then others were taken using the Impossible Project's Instant Lab. Thank you for this awesome invention.

toast collab

universal conversion chart

OVEN TEMPERATURE EQUIVALENTS

250°F = 120°C

275°F = 135°C

300°F = 150°C

325°F = 160°C

350°F = 180°C

375°F = 190°C

400°F = 200°C

425°F = 220°C

450°F = 230°C

475°F = 240°C

500°F = 260°C

MEASUREMENT EQUIVALENTS

Measurements should always be level unless directed otherwise.

⅛ teaspoon = 0.5 mL

¼ teaspoon = 1 mL

½ teaspoon = 2 mL

1 teaspoon = 5 mL

1 tablespoon = 3 teaspoons = ½ fluid ounce = 15 mL

2 tablespoons = ⅛ cup = 1 fluid ounce = 30 mL

4 tablespoons = ¼ cup = 2 fluid ounces = 60 mL

5⅓ tablespoons = ⅓ cup = 3 fluid ounces = 80 mL

8 tablespoons = ½ cup = 4 fluid ounces = 120 mL

10⅔ tablespoons = ⅔ cup = 5 fluid ounces = 160 mL

12 tablespoons = ¾ cup = 6 fluid ounces = 180 mL

16 tablespoons = 1 cup = 8 fluid ounces = 240 mL

index

NOTE: Page references in *italics* refer to photos.